# EARTHING ESSENTIALS

# EARTHING ESSENTIALS

A COMPREHENSIVE GUIDE ON GROUNDING, HARNESSING THE HEALING POWER OF NATURE, AND DEEPENING YOUR CONNECTION WITH THE EARTH

HEALING POWER OF NATURE

## NAOMI ROHAN

Teilingen
PRESS

*To my readers, may you find solace, strength, and rejuvenation in the embrace of our planet, and may your journey through this book inspire a profound and lasting reconnection with the natural world.*

*May the words within serve as a bridge, reconnecting us to the forgotten wisdom of the ground we walk upon.*

Look deep into nature, and then you will understand everything better.

— ALBERT EINSTEIN

# CONTENTS

**FREE EBOOK BY NAOMI ROHAN: Nurtured by Nature**

~~$9.99~~ **FREE EBOOK**

Scan the QR code below to download your free copy of Nurtured by Nature:

Or visit:
https://teilingenpress.wixsite.com/home/naomi-rohan

# THE CALL OF THE EARTH

Amid our bustling lives, there exists a silent whisper, a gentle call that often goes unnoticed. It is a call not heard through the ears but felt through the skin, the soles of our feet, the palms of our hands. It is a call that resonates in the marrow of our bones, in the deepest recesses of our hearts. This is the Earth's silent whisper, a subtle yet profound dialogue between the planet we inhabit and the beings we are.

The Earth, our home, is not merely a passive stage upon which the drama of life unfolds. It is an active participant, a character in its own right, with its own voice and story to tell. Yet, in our modern, technologically-driven world, we have become deaf to this voice. We have insulated ourselves with concrete and steel, rubber and plastic, and in doing so, we have severed the ancient, primal connection that once bound us to the very ground beneath our feet.

But the Earth continues to whisper, to call out to us. It beckons us to remove our shoes and step barefoot onto the grass, sand, and soil. It invites us to feel the cool dampness of morning dew, the warmth of sun-baked clay, and the rough texture of tree bark. It urges us to remember, reconnect, and ground ourselves again in the natural world.

This book explores that call, a journey into the heart of the Earth's silent whisper. It is an invitation to rekindle our relationship with the Earth, rediscover nature's healing power, and reclaim our place in the grand tapestry of life. Through the practice of earthing, we will learn to listen to the Earth's whisper, respond to its call, and find our footing on the path toward holistic healing.

## The Unseen Connection: Man and Earth

In our existence, there exists an unseen thread, a silent symphony that binds us all. It is a profound, intrinsic connection, yet often overlooked. It is the connection between man and Earth.

Imagine, if you will, standing barefoot on a lush, verdant meadow. Feel the cool, damp grass beneath your feet, the gentle hum of the Earth resonating through your soles. The sun is a warm caress on your skin, the wind a soft whisper in your ear. You are here, in this moment, and part of something much larger than yourself. You are a part of the Earth.

This connection is not merely a poetic metaphor but a tangible, physical reality. Like the Earth, our bodies are composed of myriad elements, each a testament to our shared origins. We are, in essence, children of the Earth, born of her bounty and sustained by her grace.

Yet, in our modern, fast-paced world, we have become disconnected. We have traded the soft embrace of the Earth for the cold, sterile touch of concrete. We have swapped the rhythmic pulse of nature for the relentless hum of machinery. We have lost touch with our roots, and in doing so, we have lost a part of ourselves.

But it is not too late to reclaim this connection, to rekindle this ancient bond. Through the practice of earthing, we can ground ourselves, both physically and spiritually. We can reconnect with the Earth and, in doing so, reconnect with ourselves.

This is the unseen connection between man and Earth. It is a call to return, a call to remember, a call to heal. It is a call that echoes in the silence, a call that resonates in the very core of our being. It is the call of the Earth. And it is a call that we must answer.

## Grounding Ourselves: A Journey Towards Holistic Healing

In this book, we will embark on a journey, a pilgrimage of sorts, towards a destination as old as time itself, yet as fresh and invigorating as the morning dew. This journey is not one of miles and landscapes but rather a journey of the spirit, the mind, and the body. It is a journey towards grounding ourselves, reconnecting with the Earth, and holistic healing.

The purpose of this book is to serve as a guide, a beacon of light, illuminating the path towards this profound connection. It is an invitation to step outside, to feel the Earth beneath your feet, to breathe in the air, to bask in the sunlight, and to drink from the well of life that is the Earth. It is an invitation to experience nature's healing power, to rediscover our ancestors' wisdom, and to reclaim our birthright as children of the Earth.

This book has many goals. Firstly, it aims to educate and provide a comprehensive understanding of what earthing is, its scientific basis, and its myriad benefits. It seeks to dispel myths, to challenge misconceptions, and to present the facts in a clear, accessible, and engaging manner.

Secondly, this book aims to inspire and ignite a spark of curiosity, wonder, and reverence for the Earth. It seeks to awaken a sense of belonging, interconnectedness, and responsibility towards the Earth and all its inhabitants.

Lastly, this book aims to empower and provide practical guidance on how to incorporate earthing into your daily life, cultivate a deeper connection with the Earth, and harness its healing power for physical, emotional, and spiritual well-being.

In essence, this book is a call to action, a call to return to our roots, to ground ourselves in the Earth, and to embark on a journey towards holistic healing. It is a call to listen to the Earth's silent whisper, to heed its wisdom, and to honor its gifts. It is a call to embrace the unseen connection between man and Earth and to celebrate the beauty, the mystery, and the magic of this extraordinary relationship.

**The Path Ahead: Unfolding the Layers of Earthing**

As we embark on this journey together, we will traverse the leafy valleys and towering peaks of the concept of earthing. This book is not merely a collection of words but a pathway that will guide us toward a deeper understanding of our connection with the Earth.

In the following chapters, we will delve into the history of and science behind earthing, exploring the intricate web of energy that binds us to our planet. We will examine the physiological and psychological effects of grounding, shedding light on how this simple act can profoundly change our health and well-being.

We will also explore the spiritual aspects of earthing, delving into the ancient wisdom that has long recognized the Earth's healing power. We will learn from indigenous cultures, whose practices and beliefs have been shaped by a deep reverence for the natural world.

In the latter part of the book, we will turn our attention to practical applications. We will learn how to incorporate earthing into our daily lives, whether in the heart of a bustling city or the quiet solitude of the countryside. We will discover how to create spaces in our homes and workplaces that facilitate grounding and how to make the most of our time in nature.

Finally, we will look to the future, considering the implications of earthing for our society and planet. We will reflect on the potential of grounding to foster a more sustainable, holistic way of life and to bring about a more profound sense of connection and harmony in our world.

This journey will not always be easy. It will challenge us to question our assumptions, step outside our comfort zones, and confront the disconnection that often characterizes our modern lives. But as we navigate this path together, we will find that the rewards are worth the effort. By grounding ourselves, we not only enhance our health and well-being but also contribute to the healing of our planet.

So, let us embark on this journey with open minds and hearts, ready to embrace the call of the Earth.

# 1

## THE CONCEPT OF EARTHING: A COMPREHENSIVE OVERVIEW

I n the quiet hum of the natural world, beneath the rustling leaves and the whispering winds, lies a concept as old as Earth itself. It is a concept that has been overlooked, forgotten, and often dismissed in our modern, fast-paced world. Yet, it is a concept that can transform our lives profoundly. This concept is earthing, also known as grounding, and it is the focus of our exploration in this chapter.

At its core, earthing, also known as grounding, is the practice of connecting directly with the Earth's natural electric charge. It is the act of walking barefoot on the grass, sleeping on the ground under the stars, and feeling the Earth's pulse beneath our fingertips. It is a return to our roots, a reconnection with the natural world from which we have become increasingly disconnected. The concept of earthing revolves around the idea that direct contact with the Earth's surface allows for the transfer of electrons from the ground into the body. This natural exchange is believed to promote physiological changes and healing benefits.

The simplicity of earthing lies in its accessibility. It requires no sophisticated equipment, no advanced techniques, only the willingness to step outside and make contact with the natural world. Whether through the soles of your feet, the palms of your hands, or any other part of your body, the connection is made between yourself and the Earth.

The concept of earthing is not new. It is woven into the fabric of many indigenous cultures and traditions. Yet, in our modern world, where technology reigns, and concrete jungles dominate, we have lost touch with this fundamental connection. We have insulated ourselves from the Earth with rubber-soled shoes and high-rise buildings, creating a disconnect that has far-reaching implications for our health and well-being.

In this chapter, we will unearth the concept of earthing, delving into its historical roots and the science that supports it. We will provide an overview of the various techniques and methods of earthing and the myriad health benefits it offers. We will also debunk some of the myths and misconceptions surrounding this practice, providing a comprehensive understanding of what earthing is and how it can be incorporated into our daily lives. Many of these topics will appear in later chapters of the book, allowing you to explore them in more detail.

As we embark on this journey, I hope you will approach the concept of earthing with an open mind and a willing heart, for it is in this openness, in this willingness to reconnect with the Earth, that we can truly begin to understand the healing power of earthing. So, let us begin. Let us unearth the concept of earthing, and in doing so, let us reconnect with the natural world and, ultimately, with ourselves.

## The Historical Roots of Earthing

The concept of earthing, though seemingly novel, is deeply rooted in the annals of human history. It is a practice woven into the fabric of our existence, subtly influencing our relationship with the natural world. This section aims to provide an overview of the historical roots of earthing, tracing its origins and evolution over time.

In its most primal form, the concept can be traced back to our ancestors who lived in close communion with nature. They walked barefoot, slept on the ground, and cultivated the Earth with their bare hands.

Unbeknownst to them, they practiced earthing, absorbing the Earth's energy and benefiting from its healing properties.

In ancient civilizations, the Earth was revered as a motherly presence, a source of life and healing. In many indigenous cultures around the world, the Earth was revered as a source of life and healing. The Native Americans, for instance, believed in the power of Mother Earth to heal and restore balance. They practiced earthing through their rituals and ceremonies, often involving direct contact with the Earth. Similarly, in the East, the ancient practice of yoga recognized the importance of grounding. Many yoga poses are designed to connect the practitioner with the Earth, promoting a sense of balance and tranquility.

The historical roots of earthing also extend to the realm of science. In the 18th century, the renowned scientist Benjamin Franklin conducted experiments on grounding, exploring its effects on electricity. His work laid the foundation for further research into the science of earthing.

However, as societies evolved and industrialization took hold, our connection with the Earth began to wane. Concrete jungles replaced natural landscapes, and rubber-soled shoes became the norm, severing our direct physical contact with the Earth. The practice of earthing was largely forgotten, relegated to the annals of history.

In recent years, however, there has been a resurgence of interest in earthing. This revival is fueled by a growing body of scientific research highlighting the health benefits of grounding and a broader societal shift towards holistic and naturalistic approaches to well-being.

The historical roots of earthing remind us of our innate connection with the Earth. They invite us to rediscover this connection, to return to our roots, and to embrace earthing as a holistic approach to well-being. As we delve deeper into the science and practice of earthing in the following chapters, let us keep in mind this historical perspective, grounding our understanding in the rich soil of our past.

## The Science Behind Earthing: A Closer Look

In the heart of the forest, beneath the vast, azure sky, the Earth pulses with an ancient, natural rhythm. This rhythm, this energy, is not merely a poetic metaphor but a scientific reality that forms the basis of the concept of earthing.

Imagine, if you will, the feeling of walking barefoot on a dewy stretch of grass, the sensation of sand sifting between your toes on a beach, or the solid embrace of rock underfoot on a mountain trail. These experiences are not just tactile pleasures; they are instances of earthing, moments when your body connects with the Earth's surface, tapping into its vast electrical field.

The Earth, you see, is a massive reservoir of negatively charged free electrons. These electrons are continually replenished by solar radiation, lightning, and heat from the Earth's core.

The science behind earthing lies in understanding these electrons and their interaction with the human body. Our bodies, being made up of atoms, are electrical in nature. Every heartbeat, nerve impulse, and cellular process involves the movement of electrons. It's a symphony of life conducted by nature's most fundamental particles.

When we make direct contact with the Earth, such as walking barefoot on the grass or sleeping on an earthing mat, we absorb these free electrons into our bodies. This absorption can neutralize the positively charged free radicals that are the byproducts of metabolic processes and are thought to cause inflammation and disease.

Several scientific studies support the theory. For instance, a study published in the Journal of Environmental and Public Health found that earthing changes the electrical activity in the brain, as shown by electroencephalograms. Meanwhile, other studies have shown that earthing can improve sleep, reduce pain, and decrease stress.

Earthing is also believed to influence the delicate balance of the autonomic nervous system, which controls our heart rate, digestion, respiratory rate, pupillary response, urination, and sexual arousal. This influence is because the Earth's electrons are a natural source of white noise, which can normalize biological rhythms, including circadian rhythm.

In essence, the science of earthing is a study of connections. It's about the connection between the Earth and our bodies, between the physical and the metaphysical, between the tangible world of atoms and the intangible world of energy. It's a reminder that we are not separate entities but an integral part of the universe's intricate web of life.

As we delve deeper into the science of earthing, we begin to see that it is not just a practice but a way of life, a holistic approach to well-being grounded in the universe's very fabric. It's a journey of discovery that begins with a single step, a barefoot step on the nurturing bosom of Mother Earth.

## Earthing and Human Evolution

As we delve into the intricate dance between the Earth and human evolution, we must appreciate the profound relationship that has shaped our being. The human body evolved over millions of years, and our ancestors were intimately connected to the natural world for the vast majority of that time. This connection to the Earth was not simply a matter of proximity but a fundamental aspect of their existence.

As we transitioned over generations from a nomadic lifestyle to agricultural societies and eventually to today's urbanized and technologically advanced civilizations, our direct connection with the Earth's surface slowly faded. Shoes with insulating materials, such as rubber and plastic, became the norm, and lifestyles increasingly confined people indoors.

The concept of earthing suggests that many of the health challenges faced by contemporary society, such as chronic inflammation, increased stress levels, disrupted sleep patterns, and a weakened immune response, may, in part, be a consequence of this loss of electrical contact with the Earth. By reconnecting with the Earth's surface, earthing could restore a measure of the natural balance that the course of human evolution has disrupted.

## Debunking Myths and Misconceptions about Earthing

In the realm of holistic health, earthing is a concept that has been both embraced and misunderstood. As we delve into the heart of this practice, it is essential to dispel some of the myths and misconceptions that have clouded its true essence.

One of the most prevalent misconceptions is that earthing is a new-age, pseudoscientific concept. This notion couldn't be further from the truth. Earthing, or grounding, is deeply rooted in the natural world and our ancestral connection. It is not a fleeting trend but a timeless practice that has been part of human life for millennia.

Another common myth is that earthing is merely about walking barefoot on the Earth. While this is a fundamental aspect of the practice, earthing encompasses much more. It is about fostering a deeper connection with the Earth's energy, which can be achieved through various methods, such as swimming in natural bodies of water, gardening, or even sleeping on earthing sheets.

A third misconception is that the benefits of earthing are purely psychological, a placebo effect. However, scientific studies have shown that earthing has tangible physiological effects. These include reduced inflammation, improved sleep, and enhanced wound healing. We will explore the need for further scientific research in later chapters.

Lastly, there is a myth that earthing is a cure-all solution. While earthing has numerous health benefits, it is not a panacea. It should be viewed as a complementary practice, part of a holistic approach to well-being that includes a balanced diet, regular exercise, and mental health care.

We will unpack these myths and misconceptions in a later chapter in a quest to shed light on the true nature of earthing. It is a practice rooted in our innate connection to the Earth, invites us to tap into the healing power of nature, and a practice that, combined with other healthful habits, can contribute to overall well-being.

As we move forward, let us embrace earthing for what it truly is - a natural, holistic approach to health as old as humanity itself.

**Embracing Earthing as a Holistic Approach to Well-being**

As we draw the curtain on this enlightening overview of earthing, it is essential to emphasize the holistic nature of this practice. Earthing, as we have discovered, is not merely a physical act of connecting with the Earth but a comprehensive approach to well-being that encompasses our existence's physical, emotional, and spiritual dimensions.

The Earth beneath our feet, often taken for granted, is a potent source of healing and rejuvenation. It is a silent, steadfast companion that has journeyed with us through the eons, bearing witness to our evolution, triumphs, and tribulations. By consciously reconnecting with this ancient ally through earthing, we are grounding ourselves physically and anchoring our lives in a broader, more profound context.

As we have seen, the practice of earthing is rooted in the wisdom of our ancestors, validated by modern science, and brought to life through practical techniques. It is a testament to the timeless truth that we are, in essence, children of the Earth, bound to it by the laws of nature and the rhythms of life. By embracing earthing, we acknowledge this profound connection and harness its power for our well-being.

The health benefits of earthing, ranging from improved sleep and reduced inflammation to enhanced immunity and emotional stability, are impressive. However, the true value of earthing lies not merely in these tangible outcomes, but in the subtle, transformative shifts it can bring about in our perception and experience of life. By grounding ourselves in the Earth, we are grounding ourselves in the present moment, in the here and now, which is the wellspring of holistic health and happiness.

In a world riddled with myths and misconceptions about health and well-being, earthing is a simple, natural, and accessible practice that anyone can incorporate into their lives. It is a gentle reminder that we are not separate from nature but an integral part of it and that our well-being is inextricably linked to the health of the Earth.

In conclusion, embracing earthing as a holistic approach to well-being is not just about adopting a new practice but about reclaiming ancient wisdom, rekindling a forgotten relationship, and redefining our place in the grand scheme of things. It is about coming home to ourselves, the Earth, and the interconnected web of life that sustains us all.

## Chapter Summary

- Earthing, or grounding, is the practice of connecting directly with the Earth's natural electric charge, a concept deeply rooted in many different cultures and traditions. However, modern lifestyles have led to a disconnect from this fundamental connection, impacting our health and well-being.
- The historical roots of earthing trace back to our ancestors who lived in close communion with nature. Indigenous cultures revered the Earth as a source of life and healing; even scientific studies explored the effects of grounding.
- The science behind earthing lies in understanding the Earth's negatively charged free electrons and their interaction with the human body. Direct contact with the Earth allows these electrons to flow into our bodies, neutralizing positively charged free radicals that cause inflammation and disease.
- The advent of industrialisation and urbanization and resulting disconnection from the Earth's electrical rhythms has coincided with the rise of many of the health challenges faced by contemporary society. Reconnecting with the Earth through earthing could potentially restore the natural balance that has been disrupted by the course of human evolution.
- Common misconceptions about earthing include it being a new-age concept, only about walking barefoot, its purely psychological benefits, and it being a cure-all solution. However, earthing is a timeless practice with tangible physiological effects and should be considered part of a holistic approach to well-being.

- Embracing earthing as a holistic approach to well-being is about acknowledging our profound connection with the Earth and harnessing its power for our health.
- Earthing is a simple, natural, and accessible practice anyone can incorporate into their lives. It's about reclaiming a pearl of ancient wisdom, rekindling a forgotten relationship with the Earth, and redefining our place in the interconnected web of life.

# 2

---

# EARTHING THROUGH THE AGES

Immersed in the tapestry of history, the concept of earthing and grounding emerges not as a transient trend but as a venerable tradition, rich with the echoes of ancient wisdom. Long before the term "earthing" was coined, our ancestors engaged in grounding practices, intuitively seeking the Earth's nurturing touch as a source of healing and vitality.

The ancients lived in a world where their daily lives were intertwined with the rhythms of the Earth. Their bare feet kissed the soil, they slept under the stars, and toiled with the elements in a harmonious dance of survival and spirituality. This intrinsic connection to the Earth was not incidental to their existence but a fundamental thread woven into the very fabric of their cultural and spiritual practices.

In civilizations such as those of ancient Mesopotamia, Egypt, and India, grounding was an integral part of life. The Mesopotamians revered the Earth as a bountiful giver of life. They engaged in rituals that involved direct contact with the soil, celebrating the cycles of growth and harvest. In Egypt, the connection to the Earth was embodied in their reverence for the Nile's life-giving floods and the fertile mud synonymous with regeneration and rebirth.

Across the seas, the practice of grounding in ancient India had spiritual significance. The Vedic texts, some of the oldest sacred scriptures in the world, speak of the Earth as a divine mother, "Bhumi," whose body is to be honored and cared for. Yogis and ascetics would meditate and practice yoga on the bare ground, seeking enlightenment and a profound connection with the Earth's boundless energy.

In ancient China, the notion of "Qi," or life force, was pivotal to their understanding of health and the universe. Traditional Chinese medicine emphasizes the balance of this vital energy, and grounding practices such as walking barefoot were believed to help harmonize the body's Qi with that of the Earth.

Even Greek philosophers like Aristotle and Hippocrates acknowledged the importance of the elements, including the Earth, to maintain balance and health. They championed natural therapies, including using earthen materials in medicine and walking barefoot to absorb the Earth's energies.

These ancient rituals of grounding were not only about physical health but also about maintaining a spiritual and emotional balance. The Earth was revered as a living entity, a mother who provided and sustained life. By forging a close physical connection with the ground, our ancestors believed they could tap into this life force, enhancing their wellbeing and aligning themselves with the natural order of the cosmos.

As we pivot to examining earthing in indigenous cultures, it is essential to appreciate that while grounding practices may vary across different societies and periods, the underlying principle remains the same: the Earth is a source of healing, stability, and connection that transcends cultural boundaries. The wisdom of our ancestors serves as a testament to the enduring power of this simple yet profound act of touching the Earth with our bare skin.

## Earthing in Indigenous Cultures

Throughout the tapestry of human history, the practice of earthing has woven itself into the fabric of numerous indigenous cultures around the world. These communities have long recognized the Earth as a source of healing and sustenance, not merely a physical terrain but a living entity that offers energy to all life forms.

In the lush embrace of the Amazonian rainforests, indigenous tribes have practiced walking barefoot as a way to absorb the Earth's vital energy. They believe that the soles of the feet are channels for the spirit of the Earth to enter the body and harmonize with their own life force.

Similarly, the Aboriginal peoples of Australia, with their deep spiritual connection to the land, have a concept known as "Dadirri," which translates to a profound, spiritual act of listening and quiet, still awareness. This practice involves sitting on the ground and connecting with the Earth's rhythms, a form of grounding that fosters a profound sense of peace and interconnectedness with nature.

In North America, many Native American traditions emphasize the importance of walking barefoot on the Earth to connect with the "Great Spirit." Ceremonies such as the Sundance, where flesh meets soil, are considered sacred and imbued with life-giving properties. Participants seek healing and wisdom through this intimate Earthly bond.

The Maasai of East Africa, renowned for their harmonious coexistence with nature, have long valued grounding as they stood barefoot on the Earth. They trust in the Earth's energy, absorbed through the feet, to restore physical strength and endurance, qualities essential to their nomadic lifestyle and survival.

Venturing to the Pacific, the indigenous Hawaiians have a concept called "Aloha ʻĀina," a deep love of the land. They see the land as an ancestor, a family member to be cared for and respected. They tread barefoot, anchoring themselves to lava rocks and sandy shores, to engage in a reciprocal exchange of mana, or spiritual energy, nurturing both the land and its inhabitants.

These practices, deeply rooted in the spiritual and cultural fabric of indigenous communities, affirm a universal truth: the Earth is a source of life, not just in the biological sense but as a wellspring of spiritual energy. Grounding bridges the physical and the metaphysical, a means humans have sought to align themselves with the natural world's rhythms and cycles.

As we transition to the modern world, it becomes clear that the whirl-wind of technological progress and urban sprawl has cast a shadow over the wisdom of these indigenous practices. The disconnection from the Earth's natural energy is a touching reflection of the wider disengagement from nature itself, a disconnect that influences our collective health and well-being. With this in mind, we can begin to understand the profound importance of reconnecting with the Earth, as our ancestors once did, to reclaim a sense of balance and harmony in our everyday lives.

## The Lost Connection in Modern Times

As we trace the footprints of our ancestors, we find a stark contrast in our modern lives. Our once profound connection with the Earth has become a faint echo in the cacophony of contemporary society. This disconnection is not merely symbolic but a literal separation from the electrical embrace of our planet.

In bygone eras, our predecessors walked barefoot upon the soil, slept on the ground, and cultivated the land with their hands. They existed in a perpetual embrace with the Earth's natural electrical currents, an interaction that was as much a part of life as the air they breathed.

Fast forward to the present, and our communication with the Earth has undergone a momentous shift. Modern footwear, with its insulating rubber and plastic soles, has elevated us millimeters from the Earth's surface, yet miles away from its electrical touch. Our homes, too, have become insulated islands, with floors of wood, carpet, and tile that disturb the conductive thread linking us to the ground.

The urbanization of our environments has amplified this effect. Cities, with their asphalt jungles and concrete canopies, stifle the natural flow of electrons between the Earth and our bodies. The rise of electronic devices and the presence of electromagnetic fields have created an invisible smog that further obscures our primal connection to the planet.

Our lifestyles have drifted to favor convenience and efficiency, often at the expense of our connection with nature. We spend most of our days indoors, under artificial lighting, surrounded by walls that shield us from the elemental embrace of the Earth. The simple act of walking barefoot outside has become an oddity, a relic of a bygone era viewed through nostalgia or the pursuit of leisure.

The consequences of this lost connection are not just philosophical. Emerging research hints that the lack of direct contact with the Earth's surface may have material health implications. In this context, the modern disconnection from the Earth symbolizes not just our detachment from nature but a literal gap in our physiological functioning. The insulating materials that define our modern existence—rubber, plastic, synthetic fibers—act as barriers to the Earth's natural healing potential.

At this juncture of tradition and technology, we must contemplate the impact of our choices on our health and well-being. The following section will explore the resurgence of interest in earthing as many people seek to rekindle this ancient practice and reintegrate the Earth's energy into their lives. The revival of earthing in the 21st century is not merely a trend but a collective yearning to reconnect with the source of our existence, a beckoning to rediscover the grounding force that has sustained humanity through the ages.

**Revival of Earthing in the 21st Century**

In the 21st century, a profound shift began to stir in the collective consciousness of humanity. The relentless pace of modern life began to take its toll, and a yearning for reconnection with nature's simplicity and healing rhythms began to emerge. Amidst this backdrop, the practice of earthing found new life, a revival that beckoned the weary back to the nurturing embrace of the Earth's electric heart.

This resurgence was not a sudden spark but a slow, steady flame that grew brighter as the years progressed. It was kindled by a confluence of factors: a burgeoning awareness of alternative health practices, a growing body of scientific research on the benefits of earthing, and the stories of those who had experienced profound transformations in their health and well-being.

The revival was marked by a rediscovery of the intrinsic connection between the Earth's surface and the human body. Trailblazers in earthing science began to unravel the mysteries of this connection, exploring how the Earth's natural electric charge could influence the body's physiological processes. They argued that the modern lifestyle had disturbed the electrical contact between humans and the Earth, potentially giving rise to a host of inflammation-driven ailments.

As the evidence mounted, a fresh narrative began to crystallize. The Earth emerged not as a mere stage for human endeavors but as a dynamic contributor to our vitality and well-being. Its surface, thrumming with a subtle yet potent energy, appeared to have a stabilizing effect on the body's bioelectrical landscape.

The revival of earthing in the 21st century was also a story of innovation. Visionaries and entrepreneurs saw the potential to reconnect people with the Earth's energy, even in the most urban environments. They crafted a range of new earthing products, from conductive mats and sheets to grounding footwear, allowing people to tap into the Earth's energy indoors or on the go. These products were designed to bridge the gap between the modern lifestyle and the ancient practice of earthing, making the benefits more accessible to a population largely estranged from the natural world.

The revival of earthing in the 21st century was not merely a return to an ancient practice but an evolution. It signified a merging of ancestral wisdom with modern science, acknowledging that we must not lose touch with the elemental forces that sustain us in our pursuit of advancement. As we continue navigating the complexities of contemporary life, earthing stands as a testament to the enduring human desire for connection—not just with each other but with the very ground beneath our feet.

## Earthing Movements and Communities

As we delve deeper into the historical tapestry of earthing, we find that the resurgence of interest in the 21st century has given rise to various movements and communities advocating for the practice. Though diverse in their approaches, these groups are bound by a collective appreciation for the Earth's grounding energy and have been instrumental in the revival of earthing.

A counter-movement emerged in the wake of the digital revolution, calling for a return to nature and simplicity. This movement, often called the 'Earthing Movement,' emphasizes reconnecting with the Earth's natural electrical charge. It responds to the growing scientific research suggesting that such a connection can yield significant health benefits, including reduced inflammation, improved sleep, and general well-being.

The Earthing Movement is not a monolith but a mosaic of individuals and groups, weaving their thread into the larger narrative. Among these are health and wellness practitioners who incorporate earthing into their holistic health regimes. Naturopaths, chiropractors, and massage therapists often recommend earthing with their treatments.

Another vibrant strand within the earthing tapestry is the network of online communities. These digital spaces are repositories of shared knowledge and support systems for those new to the practice. They are hubs for exchanging tips on the best earthing techniques and the most effective equipment, from grounding mats to conductive footwear.

Earthing retreats and workshops have emerged around the globe, offering immersive experiences in serene natural settings. These sanctuaries often combine earthing with other wellness practices, such as yoga, meditation, and mindful walking, to create holistic wellness packages. Participants leave grounded in the literal sense and with a deeper understanding of how to integrate earthing into their daily lives.

The Earthing Movement has also witnessed the rise of advocates and influencers who have taken to various media platforms to spread the word. Books, documentaries, and podcasts have played a significant role in popularizing the concept. These resources often feature personal testimonies, interviews with experts, and discussions on the latest research, helping to demystify earthing for the general public.

At the heart of these movements and communities lies a profound respect for the Earth and an acknowledgment of our intrinsic bond with it. This collective awareness has spurred a cultural shift that recognizes the importance of our environment not just for its resources but for its healing potential.

As these earthing communities expand, they stand at the threshold of a new epoch where the interplay of technology and nature seeks harmony. They are not merely passive participants in this age-old practice but active pioneers of a philosophy that could shape the future of human health and well-being. With feet planted firmly on the ground, these communities look forward to a future where the Earth's energy is not taken for granted but is harnessed as a vital component of living a balanced and healthy life.

## Chapter Summary

- Earthing has deep historical significance, with roots stretching back to ancient traditions and our ancestors' intuitive understanding of the Earth's healing properties.
- Ancient civilizations, including Mesopotamia, Egypt, India, China, and Greece, recognized the importance of grounding in their daily lives and spiritual practices.
- Indigenous cultures worldwide have maintained a deep connection with the Earth, viewing it as a spiritual energy and well-being source.
- The modern era has seen a disconnection from the Earth due to urbanization, insulated living, and the prevalence of synthetic materials, leading to potential health implications.
- A revival of earthing in the 21st century is driven by a growing body of scientific research and a desire to reconnect with nature for improved health and vitality.

- The resurgence of earthing has led to new products and innovations that facilitate grounding in urban environments.
- The Earthing Movement comprises health practitioners, online communities, retreats, and media influencers promoting the practice and its benefits.
- Earthing communities are growing, advocating for a balanced integration of technology and nature to harness the Earth's energy for a healthier life.

# 3

---

# THE SCIENCE BEHIND EARTHING

I n the heart of our existence, we are intimately entwined with the natural world. The air we breathe, the water we drink, and the food we eat are all gifts from Mother Earth. Yet, we often forget this primal connection in our modern, technologically driven lives. Earthing invites us to rekindle this bond, to ground ourselves in the nurturing embrace of our planet.

The human body moves to an electrical rhythm that is as essential as it is invisible. Our hearts beat thanks to electrical signals, our nervous system communicates through electrical impulses, and even our cells engage in electrical activities fundamental to their function. Within this context, we explore the relationship between electrical fields and the human body, a relationship at the heart of the practice of earthing.

Connecting directly with the Earth's surface allows us to tap into the Earth's natural, subtle electric charge. Due to countless factors, including solar and cosmic radiation and lightning hitting the Earth's surface, this charge creates a vast reservoir of negatively charged free electrons. When we make direct contact with the Earth, these electrons flow into our bodies, which has profound implications for our health and well-being.

The concept of earthing may seem simple, even primitive. Yet, it is anything but. It is a complex, fascinating interplay of physics, biology, ecology, a dance of electrons and cells, energy and matter. It is a testament to the intricate, delicate balance of life, a balance that we, as part of the web of life, are intrinsically a part of.

This chapter will delve into the science behind earthing, unraveling its mysteries and exploring its implications for human health. We will journey from the vast expanse of the cosmos to the microscopic world of our cells, from the ancient wisdom of our ancestors to the cutting-edge research of modern science.

As we embark on this journey, let us remember that earthing is not just a scientific concept or a health practice. It is a way of life, a holistic approach to well-being that invites us to reconnect with our roots, reclaim our place in the natural world, and rediscover the healing power of Mother Earth.

## The Physics of Earthing: Understanding Earth's Electromagnetic Field

In the heart of our planet, a ceaseless dance of molten iron generates a powerful electromagnetic field that envelops the Earth. This invisible yet potent force, known as the Earth's electromagnetic field, is a fundamental aspect of our planet's identity and a key player in the intriguing concept of earthing.

To comprehend the physics of earthing, we must first delve into the nature of this field. The Earth's electromagnetic field is a dynamic entity, pulsating with the rhythm of the planet's core. It extends thousands of kilometers into space, forming a protective shield against harmful solar radiation. This field is not merely a planetary defense mechanism but also a source of natural, subtle energy that permeates every inch of the Earth's surface.

Earthing, or grounding, connects our bodies to this omnipresent energy. It is as simple as walking barefoot on the grass, swimming in the sea, or touching a tree. Engaging in these activities forms a direct, physical link with the Earth's electromagnetic field. This connection allows the transfer of electrons from the Earth to our bodies, a process believed to have profound implications for our health and well-being.

The Earth's surface carries a negative electrical charge due to countless lightning strikes occurring worldwide every day. When we ground ourselves, we absorb these negative ions into our bodies. This absorption can neutralize the positive ions, or free radicals, often associated with inflammation and disease.

The physics of earthing is a fascinating blend of geophysics, biology, and chemistry. It is a testament to the interconnectedness of all things, a reminder that we are not separate entities but integral parts of a vast, complex system. It is a call to return to our roots, reconnect with the Earth, and harness its electromagnetic field's healing power.

In the following sections, we will explore the biological implications of earthing and delve into the confluence of ancient wisdom and modern science. As we journey through these topics, I invite you to keep an open mind, question, explore, and, most importantly, connect with the Earth beneath your feet.

## Biological Implications: How Earthing Influences Human Health

In the heart of nature, where the earth's pulse beats in rhythm with our own, we find a profound connection that transcends the physical. This section delves into the biological implications of earthing, exploring how this ancient practice influences human health in subtle and significant ways.

The human body, a marvel of biological engineering, is an intricate network of systems and processes working in harmony. It is a living, breathing entity constantly interacting with its environment. And the earth, with its vast electromagnetic field, is a significant part of this environment. When we engage in earthing, we immerse ourselves in this field, allowing our bodies to absorb the earth's natural, healing energy.

Our bodies are composed of many cells, each with its complex system of molecules. These molecules engage in various chemical reactions, many of which involve the exchange of electrons. Electrons are the currency of chemical reactions, facilitating the bonds between atoms and playing a pivotal role in energy production within our cells.

This transfer of electrons is made possible by the skin, our body's largest organ, which acts as a conductor, allowing us to interface with the Earth's surface. When our skin comes into contact with the ground, the Earth's electrons are believed to be absorbed into the body. These electrons have the potential to neutralize positively charged free radicals, which are known to contribute to inflammation and oxidative stress. By providing a steady stream of electrons, the Earth may act as a natural antioxidant, helping to reduce the chronic inflammation often at the root of many health disorders.

## Earthing and Inflammation

At the core of earthing's biological impact is the concept of inflammation. Inflammation, in its simplest form, is a vital part of our body's defense mechanism. However, chronic inflammation can lead to a range of health issues, from heart disease to autoimmune disorders. Earthing has been shown to reduce inflammation by neutralizing excess positive ions in the body through the influx of negative ions from the Earth, which act as natural antioxidants, combating inflammation at a cellular level.

Scientific studies have begun to shed light on the fascinating relationship between earthing and inflammation. Research utilizing thermal imaging has demonstrated that after grounding, the redness and heat associated with inflammation are reduced, indicating a reduced inflammatory response.

The implications of these findings are profound. By helping reduce chronic inflammation, earthing could aid in the prevention and management of various inflammatory diseases. It is a simple yet powerful finding that harnesses the Earth's potential to promote healing and restore balance within the body.

It is important to note, however, that while the initial research is promising, the field of earthing science is still in its infancy. The mechanisms by which grounding influences inflammation are not fully understood, and more rigorous, controlled studies are needed to substantiate these early findings and to unravel the therapeutic potential of earthing.

## Impact on Circadian Rhythms and the Nervous System

In the intricate dance of life, our bodies are attuned to the earth's natural rhythms. One of the most fundamental of these processes is the circadian rhythm, the internal clock that orchestrates our sleep-wake cycle, hormones, and eating habits, among other bodily functions. By aligning ourselves with the earth's natural rhythms, we can promote better sleep, enhance mood, and improve overall well-being.

Research suggests that earthing and grounding can influence circadian rhythms by aligning the body's internal clock with the Earth's natural electromagnetic signals. These signals are believed to act as a universal synchronizing pulse for life on our planet. Our connection to these natural rhythms has been disrupted in a modern world where exposure to artificial light and electronic devices is widespread.

By re-establishing our connection with the Earth, earthing may help recalibrate our internal clocks. The grounding effect is posited to normalize the daily cortisol rhythm, promoting better sleep, more consistent energy levels throughout the day, and a general sense of alertness and well-being.

The influence of earthing extends to the nervous system as well. The Earth's electromagnetic field can help balance the autonomic nervous system, promoting relaxation and reducing stress. This calming effect can have profound implications for mental health, offering a natural, holistic approach to managing anxiety and depression.

Earthing's impact on human health is a testament to the interconnectedness of all life. It reminds us that we are not separate entities but part of a larger world. We tap into the earth's healing energy by grounding ourselves, fostering balance and harmony within our bodies and minds.

## Unveiling the Mysteries of Earthing

As we draw this chapter to a close, it is essential to reflect on our embarked journey, exploring the intriguing science behind earthing. We have delved into the physics of our planet's electromagnetic field, the biological implications of earthing on human health, and the confluence of ancient wisdom and contemporary research.

As we have discovered, earthing is not merely a practice but a way of life, a philosophy that encourages us to reconnect with the natural world. It is a call to step away from our technologically saturated lives and ground ourselves, literally and metaphorically, in the earth beneath our feet.

The science behind earthing is compelling, suggesting that touching the earth can profoundly affect our health and well-being. It can help reduce inflammation, improve sleep, increase energy, and enhance our overall wellness. But beyond the scientific, earthing offers a deeper, more spiritual connection to the world. It reminds us that we are not separate entities but part of a vast, interconnected web of life.

Earthing provides a pathway to wholeness in a world that often feels fragmented and disconnected. It invites us to slow down, to feel the earth beneath our feet, to listen to the rhythm of nature, and to remember our place within it. It is a practice accessible to all, regardless of age, health, or location. All it requires is a willingness to step outside, feel the earth beneath our feet, and open ourselves to nature's healing power.

Earthing is more than just a scientific concept; it is a call to return to our roots, reconnect with the earth, and embrace a more grounded, holistic approach to well-being. It is a journey of discovery, a path to wellness, and a reminder of our inherent connection to the natural world. As we step forward, let us do so with our feet firmly planted on the ground, our hearts open to the wisdom of the earth, and our minds attuned to the science that unveils the mysteries of earthing.

**Chapter Summary**

- Earthing allows us to tap into the Earth's natural, subtle electric charge. This connection can be achieved through various means, such as walking barefoot on grass, lying on the beach, or using conductive systems indoors.
- The Earth's electromagnetic field is a source of natural, subtle energy that permeates every inch of the Earth's surface. When we ground ourselves, we absorb these negative ions into our bodies, which can neutralize the positive ions, or free radicals, often associated with inflammation and disease.
- Earthing has profound biological implications, including reducing inflammation, influencing our circadian rhythms, and balancing the autonomic nervous system. These effects can lead to improved sleep, enhanced mood, reduced stress, and overall better well-being.
- Modern science is exploring the ancient practice of earthing, finding that the flow of electrons from the Earth to our bodies can neutralize free radicals, alleviate inflammation, improve sleep, increase energy, and enhance overall well-being. It also suggests that earthing can help reduce stress and anxiety, improve mood, and promote a sense of calm and tranquility.
- Earthing is not just a practice but a way of life, a philosophy that encourages us to reconnect with the natural world. It offers a deeper, more spiritual connection to the world around us, reminding us that we are part of a vast, interconnected web of life.
- Embracing earthing as a holistic approach to well-being involves understanding its scientific basis, appreciating its roots in ancient wisdom, and integrating it into our daily lives. It is a journey of discovery, a path to wellness, and a reminder of our inherent connection to the natural world.

# 4

---

# EARTHING AND HEALTH: THE
# HEALING POWER OF THE EARTH

I n the grand tapestry of life, we humans are threads woven intricately into the fabric of nature. We are not separate from the Earth, but rather, we are an integral part of it. This fundamental truth, often overlooked in the hustle and bustle of modern life, forms the basis of earthing. Earthing is about re-establishing our connection with the Earth and harnessing its healing power.

This chapter will delve into the many benefits of earthing for physical and mental health. As we embark on this journey, let us remember that earthing is not just a practice but a way of life. It is a holistic approach to health and well-being that recognizes the interconnectedness of all things. It is a reminder that we are not separate from the Earth but are a part of it. And by reconnecting with the Earth, we are, in essence, reconnecting with ourselves and finding our place in the grand tapestry of life.

## Earthing and Physical Health: A Deep Dive into the Benefits

The earth beneath our feet, often taken for granted, holds a profound secret. It is a source of healing, a reservoir of energy, and a conduit for transferring life-sustaining elements. This section delves into the physical health benefits of earthing, exploring what happens to our body when we make direct contact with the earth's surface.

In its intricate design, the human body is a bioelectrical organism living in an electrical world. Our heart, brain, and nervous system are all electrical sub-systems operating within this larger system. The earth, too, is an electrical entity, pulsating with natural, subtle frequencies. Earthing, or grounding, reconnects our bodies to this natural electrical state, creating a conduit for the earth's healing energy.

One of the most significant benefits of earthing is its potential to reduce inflammation, as we explored in earlier chapters. Inflammation, often the body's response to injury, can become chronic and contribute to various health issues like heart disease, arthritis, and even cancer. The earth's surface is teeming with negatively charged electrons, and when we make direct contact with it, these electrons are absorbed into our bodies. These electrons neutralize positively charged free radicals that cause inflammation, effectively reducing it and promoting healing.

This simple act is believed to offer a natural, profound remedy for pain reduction and recovery enhancement. This is because the electrons help restore the body's natural electrical state, often disrupted by injury or illness. Preliminary studies have also shown that grounding can influence physiological processes, such as improving blood flow and viscosity, which are essential for healing and recovery.

As we also explored earlier, earthing can help improve sleep and regulate the body's circadian rhythms. The earth's magnetic field influences these rhythms, and direct contact with the earth can help synchronize our internal biological clocks with the earth's natural cycles. This synchronization can improve sleep, increase energy, and overall better health.

Finally, earthing can improve cardiovascular health. Studies have shown that grounding can normalize blood pressure and blood flow, reducing the risk of cardiovascular disease. This is likely due to the calming effect earthing has on the nervous system and the body's physiological processes. In addition, the anti-inflammatory effects of earthing can prevent cardiovascular diseases caused by chronic inflammation. By mitigating stress and its physiological repercussions, earthing may help maintain a healthier blood pressure profile.

In essence, earthing is a natural, holistic approach to health that harnesses the earth's healing power. It is a testament to the interconnectedness of all life and a reminder of our inherent bond with nature. As we delve deeper into the benefits of earthing, we begin to see the earth not just as our home but as a source of vitality, wellness, and healing.

## Earthing and Mental Well-being: The Earth's Role in Emotional Balance

In the heart of our modern, fast-paced world, where technology and artificial environments dominate, we often find ourselves disconnected from the natural world. This disconnection, some argue, has not only physical but also profound psychological implications. This section delves into the intriguing relationship between earthing and mental well-being, exploring how reconnecting with the Earth can help restore emotional balance and promote mental health.

In its infinite wisdom and timeless rhythm, the Earth has always been a source of solace and healing. It is a sanctuary where we can retreat, recharge, and realign. From a biological perspective, earthing influences the intricate dynamics of our body's electrical system. The Earth's surface is brimming with negatively charged ions, which, when absorbed into our bodies, can help neutralize harmful free radicals and reduce inflammation. This process benefits not only our physical health but also our mental state. Inflammation has been linked to various mental health disorders, including depression and anxiety. Earthing can help alleviate these conditions and promote emotional balance by reducing inflammation.

Earthing can help regulate our body's circadian rhythms and sleep quality, which are closely tied to stress and anxiety. Disruptions in this cycle can lead to sleep disorders, mood swings, and cognitive impairment. We can help reset our biological clock, improve sleep quality, and

31

enhance mood and cognitive function by grounding ourselves to the Earth.

Beyond the biological benefits, earthing also offers a psychological reprieve. It allows us to step away from the chaos of modern life and immerse ourselves in the calming embrace of nature. This immersion can help reduce stress, clear the mind, and foster a sense of peace and tranquility. It is a form of mindfulness, a way to be present in the moment and reconnect with our roots. Anecdotal evidence and preliminary studies have shown that those who practice earthing report a reduction in their stress levels and an improvement in their overall emotional well-being. They describe feeling more centered, less reactive to stressors, and more at peace.

Moreover, earthing has been shown to influence our autonomic nervous system, which controls many of our body's unconscious functions, including heart rate, digestion, and, crucially, our stress response. Studies have shown that earthing can shift our autonomic nervous system towards parasympathetic dominance, often called the 'rest and digest' state. This state is associated with feelings of calm and relaxation, a stark contrast to the 'fight or flight' response of sympathetic dominance often triggered by our modern, stressful lifestyles.

In essence, earthing is not merely a physical act but a holistic practice that nurtures our mental well-being. It is a gentle reminder of our inherent connection to the Earth, a connection that can heal, balance, and rejuvenate. As we move forward in this chapter, we will explore practical ways to incorporate earthing into our daily lives and delve into real-life experiences of its healing power.

**Reconnecting with Earth, Reconnecting with Self**

As we draw this exploration of earthing to a close, we find ourselves standing at the precipice of a new understanding, a new connection to the world beneath our feet. We have journeyed through the science and explored the physical and mental health benefits of earthing. Now, we stand ready to embrace the earth's energy in our lives and reconnect with the ground beneath us for a healthier future.

The journey we've embarked upon, from understanding the intricate workings of the human mind to the transformative power of earthing, has led us to a simple yet profound truth: reconnecting with the Earth is, in essence, reconnecting with ourselves.

In all its raw, unadulterated beauty, the Earth is not just a physical entity we inhabit. It is a living, breathing organism that we are intrinsically linked to, a symbiotic relationship that has been forgotten in our modern, technology-driven world. But as we've discovered, this connection is not merely physical. It is deeply psychological and spiritual, influencing our mental well-being in ways we are only beginning to understand.

Earthing, as we've learned, is not a complex practice reserved for the enlightened or the adventurous. It is a natural pathway to mental equilibrium, a simple act of stepping barefoot on the Earth, feeling the cool grass or the warm sand beneath our feet, and allowing the Earth's natural energy to ground us, balance us, and heal us.

Earthing is not just a practice. It's a way of life, a way of being, a way of reconnecting with the Earth, and, in doing so, reconnecting with ourselves. It's about understanding that we are not separate from the Earth, but a part of it, a part of its energy, its rhythm, its life. In this understanding, we find not just mental well-being but a sense of belonging, a sense of home, and a sense of self.

In its infinite wisdom and enduring patience, the Earth has always been there, waiting for us to remember our connection to it. It has been waiting for us to take off our shoes, feel the cool grass or the warm sand beneath our feet, and remember that we are not separate from the world but intrinsically part of it.

In reconnecting with the Earth, we are not just healing ourselves but also healing our world. We acknowledge our place in the natural order and responsibility to care for the earth as it cares for us.

As we stand on the brink of a healthier future, remember that the earth is our ally, healer, and home. Remember to walk gently, tread lightly, and honor the sacred ground beneath our feet. In doing so, we honor ourselves, our health, and the health of generations to come.

In conclusion, earthing is a practice and a way of life. It is a path to health, well-being, and a deeper understanding of our place in the world. It is a journey that begins with a single step and a moment of connection. And it is a journey that, once begun, can transform our lives in ways we never imagined. So, let us step forward, reconnect, and embrace the earth's healing power. In doing so, we embrace a healthier, more holistic future.

## Chapter Summary

- Earthing is believed to have numerous health benefits due to the Earth's natural healing power.
- Research has suggested that earthing can reduce inflammation, improve sleep and regulate the body's circadian rhythms, enhance the body's natural healing processes, and improve cardiovascular health. These benefits are attributed to the neutralization of free radicals, and the calming effect earthing has on the nervous system.
- Beyond physical health, earthing also has significant benefits for mental well-being. It can help reduce stress, clear the mind, foster a sense of peace and tranquility, and promote emotional balance. It also helps regulate our body's circadian rhythms, improving sleep quality and enhancing mood and cognitive function.
- Earthing serves as a natural pathway to mental equilibrium. By connecting with the earth, we can tap into its natural equilibrium, grounding our thoughts, quieting our emotions, and fostering a sense of inner peace.
- Earthing is not just about reconnecting with the earth but also about reconnecting with oneself. It's about grounding the

mind in the present, in the tangible reality of the earth beneath our feet, leading to greater mental well-being.

- Earthing is not a new-age fad or a fleeting trend but a return to our roots and a reconnection with the natural world. It is a recognition of the earth as a source of healing and well-being that we have too often overlooked in our modern, fast-paced lives.
- Earthing is not just a practice but a way of life. It is a path to health, well-being, and a deeper understanding of our place in the world. It is a journey that begins with a single step and moment of connection and can transform our lives in ways we never imagined.

## 5

---

# THE ART OF GROUNDING: PRACTICAL TECHNIQUES TO INCORPORATE INTO YOUR DAILY ROUTINE

T hough seemingly independent, our existence is deeply interconnected with the world around us. We are but threads woven intricately into the fabric of the universe. This intercon- nectedness extends beyond our relationships with other beings to our relationship with Earth. The Earth, our home, is not just a passive stage on which the drama of life unfolds but an active participant in our lives, offering us its energy, vitality, and healing power. This chapter invites you to embrace this energy through the practice of earthing.

As we navigate an increasingly disconnected and digital world, earthing and grounding offers a path back to our roots, a way to re-estab- lish our bond with the Earth and tap into its restorative power.

The Earth's energy is not a mystical or elusive force. It is tangible, measurable, and accessible to all. It pulses beneath our feet, courses through the air we breathe, and permeates the world around us. When we ground ourselves, we align our body's energy with that of the Earth, creating a natural balance that promotes health, wellness, and harmony.

Embracing the Earth's energy is not merely about physical contact with the ground. It is about cultivating a conscious awareness of our connection with the Earth, acknowledging its presence in our lives, and honoring its role in our well-being. It is about grounding our thoughts, emotions, and spirit as much as our physical body.

As we delve deeper into this chapter, we will explore practical techniques for daily grounding and provide guidance on different ways you can incorporate earthing into your daily life.

As you journey through these pages, may you find inspiration to embrace the Earth's energy, to ground yourself in its rhythm, and to weave this practice into the fabric of your life. For in grounding, we not only connect with the Earth, but we also connect with ourselves, with our essence, and with the universal energy that binds us all.

## Barefoot Earthing

Barefoot earthing is one of the simplest and most profound methods to reconnect with the Earth's natural electric charge. This practice involves making direct contact with the Earth's surface by walking, standing, or sitting barefoot on natural grounds such as soil, grass, sand, or even concrete, provided it is not sealed or painted.

The human body is composed of many electrical circuits, and the Earth itself is an electrical planet pulsating with a subtle yet constant electromagnetic field. The soles of our feet contain a rich network of nerves and acupuncture points, and when they make direct contact with the Earth, they allow us to absorb the Earth's electrons. These electrons are nature's anti-inflammatories, and they help to balance the body's charge, reduce inflammation, and promote physiological and electrical stability.

Barefoot earthing is not a novel or new concept. Our ancestors walked the Earth without the barrier of non-conductive materials such as rubber or plastic in modern footwear. Doing so made them naturally grounded for most of their waking hours. Today, we have largely lost this constant physical connection due to the insulating nature of our shoes and high-rise living structures.

To practice barefoot earthing, find a natural space where you feel safe and comfortable. This could be your backyard, a local park, a beach, or a forest path. Begin by simply standing still, feeling the texture and temperature of the Earth beneath your feet. Take deep breaths and allow yourself to become present in the moment. Gradually, you can start to walk gently, paying attention to the sensation of each step as your feet make contact with the ground.

As you engage in this practice, being mindful of your environment is essential. Ensure the area is free from hazards such as sharp objects, harmful organisms, or toxic substances. In an urban setting, a patch of grass or a stretch of concrete that has direct contact with the Earth can also serve as a grounding surface.

For those new to barefoot earthing, it's advisable to start with short sessions and gradually increase the duration as your body acclimates to the sensation and the practice. Some individuals may experience a tingling sensation or warmth in their feet as they ground themselves, which is a normal response as the body begins to absorb the Earth's electrons. Those who regularly practice barefoot earthing often report a sense of calmness, reduced stress levels, and an overall improvement in well-being.

Incorporating barefoot earthing into your daily routine can be as simple as taking a few moments each day to step outside and connect with the Earth. Whether it's during a morning ritual, a break in your workday, or a leisurely walk in the evening, grounding can be a powerful tool for re-establishing our connection with the natural world and enhancing our health and vitality.

As we explore the various ways to ground ourselves, it's important to remember that barefoot earthing is just one of many techniques. For those who may not have regular access to natural surfaces or for whom outdoor grounding is not practical, there are alternative methods and equipment designed to simulate the effects of earthing, which we will delve into in the following section.

## Earthing Equipment

As we transition from the tactile pleasures of barefoot earthing, where our skin directly contacts the Earth's surface, we now delve into the realm of earthing equipment. This technology is designed to provide the benefits of earthing without the need to be outdoors or in direct contact with the ground. It's particularly useful for those living in urban environments or when going barefoot outside isn't practical or possible.

Earthing equipment comes in various forms, each designed to cater to different lifestyles and preferences. Let's explore some of the most common types and how to use them effectively.

- **Earthing mats:** These are the most versatile pieces of earthing equipment. Typically made from a conductive material, such as carbon or silver mesh, these mats can be placed under your feet while working at a desk, under your keyboard and mouse, or even in bed while you sleep. To use an earthing mat, plug it into a grounded electrical outlet or connect it to a grounding rod placed directly in the Earth outside. The mat draws electrons from the ground into your body, mimicking the effect of walking barefoot on the Earth.
- **Earthing sheets and pillowcases:** For those seeking the benefits of earthing while they sleep, sheets and pillowcases embedded with conductive threads can be a game-changer. These bedding items are connected to the Earth via a grounding cord; when you lie on them, your body absorbs energy from the Earth throughout the night.
- **Earthing bands and patches:** These wearable devices can be attached to your skin at various points, such as the wrists, ankles, or over specific areas of pain. A wire connects them to a grounding point. They are handy for targeted earthing, allowing you to focus on specific areas of the body that may need attention.

- **Earthing shoes:** Innovations in footwear now allow you to stay grounded even while wearing shoes. Earthing shoes are designed with conductive materials in the sole, ensuring that you maintain an electrical connection to the Earth as you walk. They are a practical solution for those who want to practice earthing while doing their daily activities.

When using any earthing equipment, it's essential to ensure that the grounding connection is established and maintained. This typically involves a cord that plugs into a grounded outlet or a grounding rod system. It's crucial to test the outlet with a grounding checker before use in regions with electrical systems that may not be reliably grounded.

Additionally, the maintenance of earthing equipment is straightforward but necessary. Keeping the conductive surfaces clean and free from oils, sweat, and other substances that could interfere with conductivity is essential. Washing instructions vary by product, so follow the manufacturer's guidelines to preserve the effectiveness of your earthing items.

It's worth noting that while earthing equipment can be highly beneficial, like the commercialisation of any health field, they can sometimes be accompanied by unsupported marketing claims which purport false benefits. Remember that such products should complement, not replace, direct contact with the Earth. Aim to integrate barefoot earthing into your routine to embrace the grounding experience naturally and fully.

As we conclude this section, we prepare to navigate the concrete jungles where direct contact with the Earth's surface is less accessible. In the following section, we will explore strategies to stay grounded amidst the hustle and bustle of city life.

## Grounding in Different Environments: Urban, Suburban, and Wild

In the grand tapestry of life, we find ourselves woven into a myriad of environments. From the bustling heart of the city to the tranquil suburbs and even the untamed wilderness, each setting offers unique opportunities for grounding. The art of grounding is not confined to any one place; it is a practice that can be embraced wherever you find yourself.

The challenge lies in finding pockets of nature amidst the concrete jungle in urban environments. Yet, within these urban environments, the grounding connection to our planet may yield the most profound benefits, offering a respite from the electromagnetic chaos and the frenetic pace of city living. Parks, community gardens, and even tree-lined streets can serve as grounding sanctuaries. Walking barefoot on grass, hugging a tree, or simply sitting on a park bench with your hands touching the earth can help you connect with the planet's energy. Even in the most built-up areas, the Earth's energy pulses beneath us, waiting to be tapped.

Container gardening can serve as a dual-purpose activity if you have access to private outdoor spaces such as balconies or patios. Gardening is a wonderful grounding activity, allowing you to touch the earth and nurture life physically. Tending to plants and digging in the soil with your bare hands can be a grounding experience, literally and metaphorically. This practice brings you closer to the Earth and fosters a sense of presence and mindfulness. Even a small herb garden can provide an opportunity to touch the Earth through the medium of soil.

Suburban settings often provide more green spaces for grounding. Your backyard can be a grounding haven. Even a simple daily routine of walking barefoot in your yard or sitting on your porch with your feet on the ground can help you absorb the Earth's energy.

In the wild, grounding takes on a more profound dimension. Here, you are in direct contact with the raw, unfiltered energy of the Earth. Whether hiking in the mountains, camping in the forest, or walking along a beach, every step you take barefoot, every moment you spend in contact with the natural world, deepens your grounding experience.

Engaging with water can be another effective form of earthing. Many urban areas feature rivers, lakes, or coastal lines. Taking the time to wade in or touch these water bodies can help ground you. Water is a natural conductor of electricity; thus, it can facilitate the transfer of electrons from the Earth to the body.

Remember, grounding is not just about physical contact with the earth. It's also about mindfulness, being present in the moment, and acknowledging our connection with the larger ecosystem. Whether in a city apartment, a suburban home, or a cabin in the woods, take time each day to ground yourself. Feel the earth beneath you, visualize its energy flowing into you, and let it anchor you in the here and now. Remember that no matter where you are, the earth is always beneath you, ready to offer its grounding energy. Embrace it.

## Techniques for Daily Grounding: Incorporating Earthing into Your Routine

As we navigate the concrete jungles of our urban environments, it's easy to feel disconnected from the Earth's natural energy. Yet, the desire to reconnect has never been more palpable. Earthing offers a bridge to this essential connection, promising a host of health benefits we explored in the previous chapter. Now, let's focus on seamlessly integrating earthing into your daily routine.

### In the Morning

As the sun peeks over the horizon, painting the sky with hues of orange and pink, the world awakens. This is the perfect time to start your grounding journey. Begin your day with intention. Upon waking, take a moment to step outside, allowing the soles of your feet to make contact with the dew-kissed grass or the cool, moist soil.

The morning dew on the grass is not just a beautiful sight but a conduit for the Earth's energy. Walking barefoot on the dew-kissed grass is a simple yet effective grounding technique. Feel the cool wetness on your feet and the softness of the grass, and let the Earth's energy flow into you. This practice, known as 'dew walking,' is a wonderful way to start your day, aligning your body's energy with the Earth's. This simple act can help set a grounded tone for the day ahead. If you have a garden or backyard, consider creating a small barefoot path with stones, grass, or sand to enhance this morning ritual.

## During the Day

As the day progresses, take short grounding breaks. If you work in an office, take a break to step outside, remove your shoes, and place your feet on the ground. If you're at home, step outside and connect with the Earth. Even a few minutes of grounding can help reset your energy and reduce stress.

During lunch, consider eating outside. Eating is inherently grounding, connecting us to the Earth's bounty. By eating outdoors, you can enhance this connection. Feel the sun on your skin, the breeze in your hair, and the Earth beneath you as you nourish your body.

## In the Evening

In the evening, grounding can help you do the same as the world begins to wind down. A walk in nature, if accessible, can be an excellent way to end the day. A park or tree-lined street can provide a grounding experience if you live in an urban environment. Pay attention to the sensation of the ground beneath your feet, the rustling of leaves in the wind, and the chirping of birds returning to their nests. These simple observations help you connect with the Earth and ground your energy.

Before bed, consider a grounding meditation. Visualize roots growing from your feet, reaching deep into the Earth, anchoring you. Feel the Earth's energy flowing up these roots, filling your body with calm and stability. This practice can help you release the day's stress and prepare for a restful night's sleep.

## Other Ways to Embrace Earthing

Make earthing a family affair. Encourage your loved ones to join you in grounding activities. This could be as simple as walking barefoot in the park together or as engaging as a family gardening project. Not only does this promote health and well-being for everyone involved, but it also strengthens your collective bond with nature and each other.

Travel with grounding in mind. When you're on the road, seek opportunities to connect with the Earth. This could be a walk on the beach, a hike in the forest, or simply finding a patch of grass in a rest area. Portable grounding mats and bands are also available when direct contact with the Earth isn't possible.

For those who enjoy physical activity, consider grounding exercises such as yoga or Tai Chi performed outdoors on the earth's surface. These practices combine the benefits of movement, mindfulness, and grounding in a powerful synergy that can enhance your physical and mental health.

Lastly, practice mindfulness with earthing. As you ground yourself, be present in the moment. Feel the texture of the Earth beneath your feet, the temperature, the moisture. Breathe deeply and acknowledge the subtle energies at play. This mindfulness aspect can enhance the Earthing experience, creating a meditative practice that nurtures both body and soul.

Grounding is not a one-size-fits-all practice. It is a personal journey that you can tailor to your lifestyle and needs. The key is to be mindful, present, and connect with the Earth in a way that feels right for you. By incorporating grounding techniques into your daily routine, from morning to night, you're reconnecting with the Earth's natural rhythms and investing in your long-term well-being.

## The Path Forward with Grounding Practices

As we draw this exploration of grounding to a close, it is essential to remember that the journey towards embracing the Earth's energy is not a destination but a continuous process. The path forward with grounding practices is not a straight line but a winding trail that meanders through the landscapes of our daily lives, inviting us to pause, connect, and immerse ourselves in the natural world.

In holistic health, grounding is a gentle yet powerful tool, a bridge that connects us to the Earth and ourselves. It is a practice that invites us to slow down, feel the Earth beneath our feet, and listen to life's subtle rhythms. It is a reminder that we are not separate from the world around us but rather a part of it, woven into the very fabric of life.

The Earth beneath our feet pulses with a natural energy, a gentle current that hums with life and vitality. This energy, often overlooked in our modern, fast-paced lives, has the potential to nourish and rejuvenate us in ways we are only beginning to understand. Grounding allows us to tap into this reservoir of vitality, to draw strength and serenity from the very soil we walk upon.

Incorporating earthing into your daily life does not require drastic changes. It is about making small, mindful adjustments, about taking moments to disconnect from the artificial and reconnect with the natural. It is about grounding your mind in the present, in the tangible reality of the earth beneath your feet. And in doing so, you may find a path to greater mental well-being, a sense of calm and balance rooted in the earth itself.

Earthing is not merely a technique or a tool but a way of life. It is a conscious choice to engage with the Earth's energy, root ourselves in the present moment, and cultivate a deep connection with the world around us. It is a commitment to nurturing our holistic health and wellness and fostering a sense of balance and harmony within ourselves and the environment.

As we move forward, let us remember that grounding is a journey of discovery that invites us to explore, experiment, and experience. It is a journey that encourages us to step outside our comfort zones, challenge our preconceived notions, and question our assumptions. It is a journey that beckons us to venture into the unknown, to delve into the depths of our being, to unearth the treasures that lie within.

In the end, grounding is not about mastering a technique or achieving a goal. It is about cultivating relationships with the Earth, ourselves, and the world. It is about living in harmony with the natural rhythms of life, about embracing the ebb and flow, the rise and fall, the dance of existence. It is about grounding ourselves in the essence of who we are and what it means to be alive. And in this grounding, we find not only a path forward but a homecoming, a return to our true nature, a return to the Earth.

## Chapter Summary

- Barefoot earthing involves making direct contact with the Earth's surface by walking, standing, or sitting barefoot on natural grounds, such as soil, grass, sand, or even concrete, to absorb the Earth's electrons.
- Earthing equipment is designed to provide the benefits of earthing without the need to be outdoors or in direct contact with the ground. Such equipment is particularly useful for those living in urban environments or when going barefoot outside isn't practical or possible.
- Grounding can be practiced in various environments, from urban to suburban to wild. Each setting offers unique opportunities for grounding, from parks in the city to gardening in the suburbs to hiking in the wilderness.
- Grounding can be practiced throughout the day, from walking barefoot on dew-kissed grass in the morning to grounding meditation before bed. These practices can help reset energy, reduce stress, and prepare for a restful night's sleep.
- Practicing mindfulness when grounding can enhance the earthing experience, creating a meditative practice that nurtures both your body and soul.
- By incorporating grounding techniques into your daily routine, you're reconnecting with the Earth's natural rhythms and investing in your long-term well-being.
- The journey towards embracing the Earth's energy is continuous. The path forward with grounding practices is a

winding trail that invites us to pause, connect, and immerse ourselves in the natural world.

- Grounding is about cultivating a relationship with the Earth, ourselves, and the world. It is about living in harmony with the natural rhythms of life and grounding ourselves in the essence of who we are.

# 6

PERSONAL STORIES:
TRANSFORMATIVE EXPERIENCES
WITH EARTHING

I n the vast tapestry of human experience, stories serve as threads, weaving together the intricate patterns of our lives. They are the vessels that carry our truths, lessons, and wisdom. They are the mirrors that reflect our shared humanity. Personal narratives hold a unique and potent power in the realm of earthing. They illuminate the transformative effects of this simple yet profound practice, grounding us in the tangible reality of our connection with the Earth.

Earthing, the act of making direct physical contact with the surface of the Earth, is a practice as old as humanity itself. Yet, in our modern, technology-driven world, it is a practice that has been largely forgotten, overlooked, or dismissed. But the stories of those who have rediscovered earthing and felt its healing touch tell a different tale. They speak of returning to our roots, reconnection with our natural environment, and rekindling our innate capacity for healing and wholeness.

These narratives are not just stories of personal transformation. They are also stories of awakening, a dawning awareness of our place within the larger web of life. They are stories of healing, of the body's remarkable ability to repair and regenerate itself when given the chance. They are stories of emotional and psychological growth, of finding peace, balance, and resilience in the face of life's challenges. They are stories of spiritual journeys, of a deepening sense of purpose and meaning. And they are stories of community, of the ripple effects of one person's transformation on their relationships and broader social circles.

In this chapter, we will delve into these personal narratives, exploring how earthing has touched and transformed lives. We will journey with individuals as they recount their first encounters with earthing, their experiences of physical recovery, their emotional and psychological transformations, their spiritual awakenings, and the impact of their earthing practice on their relationships and communities.

Through these stories, we will understand the power of earthing as a practice and a way of life. In vivid detail, we will see the potential that lies in each of us to reconnect with the Earth, heal, grow, and transform. And perhaps, in the process, we will be inspired to write our own earthing story.

## The Awakening: First Encounters with Earthing

In the stillness of the early morning, as the sun's first rays gently kiss the dew-kissed grass, a profound connection occurs when bare feet touch the Earth. This is the awakening, the first encounter with earthing, a moment that has marked the beginning of a transformative journey for many.

For some, this awakening is a sudden, electrifying jolt, a palpable surge of energy that courses through the body, grounding and invigorating them in ways they had never experienced before. It's as if the Earth, in its silent wisdom, has reached out and touched their soul, sparking a connection that feels as ancient as the planet itself.

For others, the awakening is a slow, gentle unfurling, a gradual realization of the subtle shifts occurring within their bodies and minds. It's a soft whisper in the wind, a soothing lullaby sung by the rustling leaves, a comforting embrace that wraps around them, seeping into their bones, blood, and being. It's a sense of coming home, being cradled by the Earth, being part of something larger, something timeless.

These first encounters with earthing are as diverse as the individuals who experience them, yet they all share a common thread - a profound sense of connection and transformation. They speak of a newfound awareness, a deep-seated respect for the Earth and its healing powers, and a sense of peace and balance that permeates every aspect of their lives.

Take, for instance, the story of a middle-aged woman, a corporate executive, who stumbled upon earthing during a wellness retreat. Her first encounter was nothing short of a revelation. As she stood barefoot on the dewy grass, she felt a surge of energy, a sense of calmness washing over her like a gentle wave. It was a moment of pure, unadulterated connection that marked the beginning of her journey towards holistic healing and wellness.

Or consider the tale of a young man, a college student battling anxiety and depression, who discovered earthing through a friend. His first experience was subtle, almost invisible. Yet, over time, he noticed a shift, a gradual easing of his anxiety, a sense of peace that seemed to radiate from the ground beneath his feet. It was a slow awakening, a gentle nudge toward healing and self-discovery.

These stories, and countless others, serve as powerful testaments to the transformative potential of earthing. They remind us of the profound connection we share with the Earth, a connection that has the power to heal, transform, and awaken the deepest parts of our being.

## The Healing Ground: Stories of Physical Recovery through Earthing

In the grand tapestry of life, the Earth beneath our feet often goes unnoticed, yet it holds a profound potential for healing. This section is a testament to the transformative power of earthing, as told through the personal narratives of those who have experienced physical recovery through this practice.

Our first story is that of Sarah, a marathon runner from Colorado. A stress fracture had sidelined her, causing not only physical pain but also a deep sense of frustration and loss. It was during this period of recovery that she discovered earthing. Sarah began to spend time barefoot in her garden, allowing the soles of her feet to connect with the cool, damp Earth. She described the sensation as a gentle, grounding energy that seemed to flow into her, soothing her pain and calming her restless spirit. Over time, her fracture healed, but more than that, she found a new sense of balance and connection.

Then there is James, a retired teacher from Maine, who suffered from chronic insomnia. Nights were long, lonely vigils until he started earthing. He began with simple walks on the beach, feeling the wet sand beneath his feet, the rhythmic pulse of the ocean echoing in his heartbeat. Gradually, his sleep patterns normalized. He attributed this change to the Earth's natural frequencies, which he believed helped regulate his body's rhythms.

In the heart of New York City, we find Maya, a corporate executive who was diagnosed with hypertension. The frenetic pace of her life seemed to echo in her racing heart until she found solace in a small city park. She started spending her lunch breaks there, sitting barefoot on the grass, feeling the steady, reassuring presence of the Earth beneath her. Over time, her blood pressure readings normalized. She felt a sense of calm she hadn't experienced in years.

These stories, and many others, paint a vivid picture of the healing potential of earthing. They show us that the Earth, in its silent, enduring way, offers us a sanctuary of healing and recovery. It invites us to step off the concrete, feel the soil, grass, and sand beneath our feet, and tap into the restorative power that lies beneath the surface.

The following sections will explore the emotional, psychological, and spiritual transformations brought about by earthing. As we delve deeper into these personal narratives, we will discover that the healing ground is not just about physical recovery. It is about reconnecting with our natural environment and rediscovering our place. It is about grounding ourselves in the present moment and finding harmony within ourselves and the world around us.

**The Earth's Embrace: Emotional and Psychological Transformations**

At the heart of our narrative journey, we delve into the profound emotional and psychological transformations that earthing can initiate. In its infinite wisdom and quiet strength, the Earth can cradle us in its embrace, offering solace and healing to our weary souls.

The stories in this section are as varied as the individuals who share them. Yet, they all speak of a deep, almost primal connection to the Earth that transcends the physical, reaching into the very core of our emotional and psychological being.

One such narrative is that of Nina, a woman who had been grappling with anxiety and depression for most of her adult life. Traditional therapies and medications provided temporary relief, but the darkness always found a way to creep back in. It was only when she discovered earthing that she experienced a profound shift.

Walking barefoot in her garden, feeling the cool, damp soil beneath her feet, Nins felt a sense of calm she hadn't experienced in years. The Earth, she said, absorbed her anxiety, her fears, and her sadness like a sponge soaking up water. Over time, her connection with the Earth became her sanctuary and healing place. The Earth's embrace became her therapy, grounding her emotions and thoughts and allowing her to experience life with a newfound sense of peace and balance.

Then there's the story of Ryan, a war veteran haunted by the ghosts of his past. His companions were nightmares, flashbacks, and a constant sense of unease until he stumbled upon earthing. The simple act of standing barefoot on the Earth, feeling its steady pulse beneath his feet, began to soothe his troubled mind. The Earth, he said, didn't judge or demand; it simply was. This acceptance, this unconditional embrace, allowed him to process his trauma and find a semblance of peace amidst the chaos.

These stories, and countless others, illustrate the profound emotional and psychological transformations that earthing can facilitate. They remind us that we are not separate from the Earth but intrinsically

NAOMI ROHAN

connected to it. And in this connection, in the Earth's quiet, unassuming embrace, we can find healing, peace, and transformation.

## The Harmonious Connection: Spiritual Journeys Initiated by Earthing

In the heart of our existence lies a profound longing for connection, a yearning to be part of something greater than ourselves. This longing often leads us on spiritual journeys, quests for meaning and purpose that transcend the mundane and the material. For many, earthing has catalyzed such journeys, opening up new pathways of understanding and experience that resonate deeply with the soul.

The stories in this section are a testament to the transformative power of earthing on a spiritual level. They are tales of individuals who have discovered a sense of unity and harmony that extends beyond the physical realm through their direct contact with the Earth.

One such story is that of Beth, a woman in her mid-thirties who had spent most of her life feeling disconnected and adrift. Despite her successful career and seemingly perfect life, she felt an emptiness within that she couldn't quite understand. It was only when she stumbled upon the practice of earthing during a wellness retreat that she experienced a profound shift.

Walking barefoot on the dew-kissed grass, she felt a surge of energy coursing through her, a sensation she described as "coming home." This was not just a physical sensation but a spiritual awakening. She felt a deep sense of belonging, a connection to the Earth and the universe she had never experienced before.

In the silence of the early morning, with the Earth beneath her feet and the sky above her, Beth found a sense of peace and wholeness that had eluded her for years. She began to see herself not as an isolated entity but as an integral part of the web of life. This realization sparked a spiritual journey that transformed her life, leading her to a deeper understanding of herself and her place in the world.

Beth's story is not an isolated one. Many others have embarked on similar spiritual journeys initiated by earthing, finding in practice a bridge between the physical and the spiritual, the self and the universe. They have discovered a harmonious connection that has enriched their lives, bringing peace, purpose, and profound joy.

In the grand tapestry of existence, we are all interconnected threads woven together by the energy of the Earth. Through earthing, we can tap into this energy, grounding ourselves in the present moment and opening ourselves up to the spiritual dimensions of our being. As these personal stories illustrate, the journey may be deeply personal, but the destination is universal: a harmonious connection with the Earth, ourselves, and the cosmos.

## The Ripple Effect: How Earthing Transformed Relationships and Communities

The practice of earthing is not an isolated phenomenon. It ripples out, touching the individual and the relationships and communities around them. This section explores the transformative power of earthing as it extends beyond the self, reshaping relationships and revitalizing communities.

The stories shared here are as diverse as the people who tell them, yet they all echo a common theme: earthing has a profound capacity to foster connection. It begins personally with the individual forming a deep, grounding bond with the Earth. This connection, in turn, influences their interactions with others.

Consider the story of Marianne, a mother of two from Colorado. She discovered earthing during a period of personal turmoil. As she began to spend time barefoot in her garden, she noticed a shift in her mood and energy levels. This newfound calm and vitality had a ripple effect on her family life. Inspired by her example, her children began to join her in the garden. The shared experience of earthing brought them closer, fostering a sense of unity and mutual understanding that had been missing in their relationship.

Similarly, a community found unity through earthing in the small coastal town of Astoria, Oregon. Once a neglected space, the local park became a hub for earthing enthusiasts. As more people began to gather, barefoot and open-hearted, the park transformed into a vibrant community space. The practice of earthing became a shared language, bridging gaps between generations and backgrounds. It fostered a sense of belonging, a connection to the Earth and each other.

These stories illuminate the transformative power of earthing as it ripples outwards, touching relationships and communities. They remind us that earthing is not just a solitary practice but a collective experience. It is a shared journey of grounding, healing, and connection. As we connect with the Earth, we also connect with each other, creating a profound ripple effect that can transform our relationships and communities.

In the next section, we will reflect on the personal and collective impact of earthing, drawing together the threads of these personal narratives to understand the broader implications of this practice.

### Reflecting on the Personal and Collective Impact of Earthing

As we draw this chapter close, we find ourselves standing on the precipice of understanding, looking out over the vast spectrum of personal and collective transformation that earthing has brought about. The stories we've shared are tales of individual awakening, healing, and spiritual growth, as well as narratives of community bonding and societal change.

Earthing, as we've seen, is not merely a practice. It is a way of life, a philosophy that encourages us to reconnect with the natural world, ground ourselves in the Earth's energy, and find balance and harmony within ourselves and others. The personal impact of earthing is profound, as evidenced by the stories of physical recovery, emotional healing, and spiritual awakening.

But the power of earthing extends beyond the individual. It ripples outwards, touching those around us, transforming relationships, and fostering community. It encourages us to slow down, be present, and listen to our bodies, the Earth beneath our feet, and the people around us. It teaches us to respect and care for the natural world, to recognize our place within it, and to understand that our health and well-being are intrinsically linked to the health and well-being of the planet.

The collective impact of earthing is best seen in the growing movement towards sustainable living and environmental stewardship. As more and more people discover the benefits of earthing, they are also becoming more aware of the need to protect and preserve the natural world. This shift in consciousness is leading to changes in behavior, from the choices we make as consumers to the policies we support as citizens.

In reflecting on the personal and collective impact of earthing, we are reminded of the interconnectedness of all things. We are part of the Earth, and the Earth is part of us. Our stories are woven into the fabric of the planet, and the planet's story is woven into us. Through earthing, we are grounding ourselves physically, emotionally, psychologically, and spiritually. We are finding our place in the world, and in doing so, we are helping to shape a more balanced, harmonious, and sustainable future.

**Chapter Summary**

- Personal narratives illuminate the profound, transformative effects of earthing, which involves making direct physical contact with the Earth. These stories highlight this practice's healing and grounding effects, which are largely overlooked in our modern, technology-driven world.
- First encounters with earthing can be powerful and transformative, sparking a deep connection with the Earth that can be refreshing and calming. These experiences often mark the beginning of a journey towards holistic healing and wellness.
- Earthing has the potential to aid physical recovery. Stories of individuals who have experienced healing from conditions

like stress fractures, insomnia, and hypertension through earthing underscore the Earth's restorative power.

- The practice of earthing can facilitate profound emotional and psychological transformations. Earthing can help individuals find peace, balance, and healing by grounding their emotions and thoughts.
- Earthing can initiate spiritual journeys, fostering a sense of unity and harmony that extends beyond the physical realm. Through earthing, individuals can experience a deep sense of belonging and connection to the universe.
- The practice of earthing can have a ripple effect, transforming not only the individual but also their relationships and communities. Shared experiences of earthing can foster unity, mutual understanding, and a sense of belonging.
- The collective impact of earthing is seen in the growing movement towards sustainable living and environmental stewardship. As more people discover the benefits of earthing, they become more aware of the need to protect and preserve the natural world.
- The personal and collective impact of earthing reminds us of the interconnectedness of all things. Through earthing, we are grounding ourselves physically, emotionally, psychologically, and spiritually, helping to shape a more balanced, harmonious, and sustainable future.

# 7

## EARTHING ACROSS CULTURES: A GLOBAL PERSPECTIVE

E arthing is a universal language, spoken not in words but in the silent communion between the soles of our feet and the soil beneath them. This language transcends geographical boundaries, cultural differences, and historical epochs, uniting us all in a shared experience of the Earth's grounding energy.

In its infinite wisdom, the Earth has been whispering to us since the dawn of time. It has been telling us stories of life and death, growth and decay, and the eternal cycle of seasons. It has taught us balance, harmony, resilience and regeneration. And it has been inviting us to join this grand symphony of life, to become active participants in the unfolding drama of the natural world.

Earthing is our response to this invitation. It is our way of saying 'yes' to the Earth, acknowledging our place in the grand scheme of things, and embracing our role as stewards of this beautiful planet. It is our way of tuning into the Earth's frequency, aligning our rhythms with the rhythms of nature, and grounding ourselves in the here and now.

Earthing is not a new concept nor exclusive to any particular culture or tradition. It is a universal practice rooted in our shared human experience. From the indigenous tribes of the Amazon rainforest to the nomadic herders of the Mongolian steppes, from the yogis of ancient India to the philosophers of classical Greece, from the shamans of Africa to the scientists of the modern West, people from all walks of life and all corners of the globe have been practicing earthing in one form or another.

This chapter will take you on a journey around the world, exploring how different cultures have interpreted and practiced earthing. It will delve into the deep-rooted connection between indigenous cultures and the Earth, the Eastern philosophies that view earthing as a way of harnessing the energy of life, the Western scientific approach to earthing, and the African traditions that see earthing as a spiritual practice. It will also look at the modern revival of earthing and what the future might hold for this ancient practice.

So, let's embark on this journey together, exploring the universal language of earthing and discovering how it can help us connect with the Earth, each other, and ourselves.

## Earthing in Indigenous Cultures: A Deep-rooted Connection

In the heart of the world's most ancient cultures, the practice of earthing, or grounding, is not a novelty or a trend but a way of life deeply woven into their existence. Indigenous cultures, from the Aboriginal tribes of Australia to the Native Americans of North America, have long recognized the Earth as a living entity, a source of life, and a conduit for healing and spiritual connection.

For instance, the Aboriginal people of Australia have a profound relationship with the land that transcends the physical. Their Dreamtime stories speak of the Earth as a sacred mother, a provider, and a spiritual guide. Walking barefoot on the Earth, sleeping on the ground, and participating in ceremonies that connect them to the land are integral parts of their culture. This intimate connection with the Earth, this practice of earthing, is believed to maintain their physical health and spiritual well-being and to keep them in harmony with the cycles of nature.

Similarly, Native American cultures have a rich tradition of earthing.

The Earth is revered as a powerful spiritual entity, and many rituals and ceremonies involve direct contact with the Earth. Sweat lodges, for example, are built directly on the Earth, and participants sit on the ground inside, connecting with the Earth's energy as they purify and heal. The practice of earthing is also evident in their daily life, from walking barefoot to sleeping on the Earth.

In these cultures, earthing is not merely a physical act but a holistic practice encompassing the body, mind, and spirit. It is a way of grounding oneself in the present, connecting with the energy of life that pulses beneath our feet, and acknowledging our place in the vast web of life that the Earth supports.

Though varied in their specifics, these indigenous practices of earthing share a common understanding: that the Earth is a source of healing, energy, and spiritual connection. They remind us that we are not separate from the Earth but a part of it and that by connecting with the Earth, we connect with ourselves and the greater whole. As we delve deeper into the practice of earthing, we find that this ancient wisdom holds profound relevance for our modern lives, offering a path to health, balance, and a more profound sense of connection with the world around us.

**Eastern Philosophies: Earthing and the Energy of Life**

In the East, the concept of earthing and grounding is not novel. It is deeply embedded in their philosophies and way of life, intertwined with the fundamental principles of energy and balance. The Eastern philosophies, particularly those of China, India, and Japan, have long recognized the Earth as a source of life-giving energy, a conduit for healing, and a medium for spiritual connection.

In Chinese philosophy, 'Qi' or 'Chi' is central. It is the life force or energy flow that permeates everything in the universe. In this context, the Earth is seen as a reservoir of this vital energy. Walking barefoot, practicing Tai Chi in nature, or meditating outdoors are ways to connect with the Earth's energy, balance one's Qi, and promote physical and emotional well-being.

Similarly, in Indian philosophy, the Earth is revered as 'Prithvi' or 'Bhumi,' the goddess of the Earth. The practice of yoga, particularly 'Hatha Yoga,' encourages a deep connection with the Earth. The term 'Hatha' combines 'Ha,' meaning sun, and 'Tha,' meaning moon, symbolizing the balance of energies. Many yoga asanas or postures are designed to ground the practitioner, to help them draw energy from the Earth, and to create a harmonious flow of life force or 'Prana' within.

In Japan, the practice of 'Shinrin-yoku' or 'forest bathing' is a testament to the Japanese belief in the healing power of nature. It is a practice of immersing oneself in the forest, of connecting with the Earth through all five senses. The Earth, the trees, and the air are all seen as sources of 'Ki,' the universal energy.

These Eastern philosophies, with their emphasis on the energy of life, offer a holistic approach to earthing. They see the Earth not just as a physical entity but as a spiritual and energetic one. They recognize that our relationship with the Earth is not merely physical but deeply energetic and spiritual. They teach us that by grounding ourselves and connecting with the Earth, we can balance our energies, enhance our well-being, and deepen our understanding of ourselves and the universe.

In the next section, we will explore the Western perspectives on earthing, where the focus shifts from the spiritual and energetic to the scientific and empirical.

**Western Perspectives: The Scientific Approach to Earthing**

In the West, the concept of earthing and grounding has been approached with a scientific lens. This perspective, while different from other cultures' spiritual and philosophical interpretations, is no less profound in its implications.

The scientific exploration of earthing began in earnest in the late 20th century, with researchers seeking to understand the physiological effects of direct physical contact with the Earth's surface. The Earth, they discovered, is a vast reservoir of negatively charged free electrons. When a human body makes direct contact with the Earth, these electrons are absorbed, stabilizing the body's bioelectrical environment, as we learned in earlier chapters.

This discovery led to a series of studies examining the potential health benefits of earthing. The results were intriguing. Regular grounding, researchers found, could reduce inflammation, improve sleep, increase energy, lower stress, and enhance the body's healing processes. These findings provided a scientific basis for the intuitive wisdom of indigenous cultures, who have long recognized the Earth's healing power.

Yet, the Western approach to earthing is not without its critics. Some argue that the focus on physiological benefits overlooks the practice's deeper, more holistic aspects. Earthing, they contend, is not just about absorbing electrons but about reconnecting with the natural world, grounding oneself in the present moment, and fostering a sense of belonging to the more extensive web of life.

Despite these debates, the scientific exploration of earthing has played a crucial role in its global resurgence. It has brought the practice into the mainstream, sparking interest among health professionals, wellness enthusiasts, and the general public. It has also opened up new avenues for research, with scientists now investigating the potential of earthing to treat various health conditions, from chronic pain to cardiovascular disease.

Ultimately, the Western perspective on earthing offers a compelling blend of ancient wisdom and modern science. It reminds us that, despite our technological advances, we are still creatures of the Earth, bound by its rhythms and sustained by its energies. And it invites us to explore this connection, not just as a path to better health but as a way of living more fully, consciously, and harmoniously with the world around us.

## African Traditions: Earthing as a Spiritual Practice

In Africa's vast and diverse continent, the practice of earthing and grounding is not merely a physical act but a spiritual journey. It is a sacred ritual, a conduit for connecting with the ancestors, the Earth, and the divine. The African perspective on earthing is deeply rooted in the belief that the Earth is a living, breathing entity, a source of life and wisdom, and a spiritual guide.

In many African cultures, the Earth is revered as a mother figure, a nurturing entity that provides sustenance, protection, and wisdom. The act of earthing and making direct contact with the Earth is seen as a way of tapping into this wisdom, of drawing strength and guidance from the Earth. It is a practice often incorporated into spiritual rituals and ceremonies, grounding the participants and connecting them with the spiritual realm.

In the Yoruba culture of West Africa, for instance, the Earth is personified as the goddess Ile, the mother of all beings. Ile is revered as a source of wisdom and guidance, and the act of earthing is seen as a way of communing with her, of seeking her counsel. During spiritual ceremonies, participants often touch the Earth, a symbolic act of reaching out to Ile and seeking her blessing and guidance.

Similarly, in the Zulu culture of South Africa, the Earth is seen as a spiritual entity, a source of life and wisdom. The act of earthing is incorporated into many spiritual rituals, connecting with the ancestors and seeking their guidance and protection. It is a practice deeply ingrained in the culture, a testament to the enduring connection between the people and the Earth.

In these cultures, and many others across the continent, earthing is not merely a physical act but a spiritual practice, a way of connecting with the divine, seeking guidance and wisdom. It is a practice deeply rooted in the culture, a testament to the enduring connection between the people and the Earth.

As we explore the practice of earthing across cultures, it becomes clear that it is more than just a physical act. It is a spiritual journey, a way of connecting with the Earth, the divine, and ourselves. It is a practice that transcends cultural boundaries, a universal language that speaks to our innate need for connection, grounding, and a sense of belonging. It is a practice that remains, at its core, a shared ground despite its many interpretations and manifestations.

### Global Trends: The Modern Revival of Earthing

A quiet revolution is taking place in the heart of our technologically driven world. It is a movement that is not about advancing further into the digital age but rather about returning to our roots, to the Earth beneath our feet. This is the modern revival of earthing, a global trend reconnecting individuals with the natural world.

The modern revival of earthing is not a sudden phenomenon. It is a gradual awakening, a slow but steady realization of the importance of our connection with the Earth. It is a response to the increasing disconnection we feel in our fast-paced, urbanized lives, where concrete and screens often replace grass and skies.

This trend is not confined to any one region or culture. From the bustling cities of Tokyo and New York to the tranquil countryside of Tuscany and the rugged landscapes of Australia, people are rediscovering the grounding effects of direct contact with the Earth. They walk barefoot in parks, practice yoga on the beach, garden with their hands, and sleep on earthing sheets. They are seeking out these experiences not just for the physical benefits but also for the mental and emotional balance they bring.

A growing body of scientific research also fuels the modern revival of earthing. Studies reveal the potential impact of earthing on everything from sleep quality and stress levels to inflammation and pain management. This scientific validation is helping to bridge the gap between ancient wisdom and modern understanding, making earthing more accessible and appealing to a broader audience.

But perhaps the most powerful driver of this trend is the personal experiences of those who practice earthing. The stories of transformation and healing, peace and clarity inspire others to try earthing for themselves. They prove that in a constantly changing and evolving world, some things remain constant. The Earth beneath our feet is one of them.

As we look to the future, the modern revival of earthing shows no signs of slowing down. It is a testament to our innate need for connection, not just with each other but with the Earth itself. It is a reminder that no matter where we come from or where we are going, we all share the same ground. And that is a powerful message in a world that can often feel divided.

## The Future of Earthing - A Shared Ground

As we draw this global exploration of earthing to a close, we find ourselves standing on a shared ground, a common soil that binds us all, regardless of our cultural, geographical, or philosophical differences. The future of earthing is a future of unity and shared understanding, a future where the wisdom of the ancients meets the discoveries of modern science and where the spiritual meets the physical in a harmonious dance of energy and connection.

The resurgence of earthing in contemporary society is a testament to our innate longing for connection, not just with each other but with the natural world surrounding and sustaining us. As we move forward, this connection will guide us, grounding us in the wisdom of the Earth and the energy of life itself.

In the West, scientific research continues to uncover the tangible benefits of earthing, validating what indigenous cultures and Eastern philosophies have known for centuries. The Earth's energy profoundly impacts our physical and mental well-being. As we continue to explore this connection, we can expect to see a greater emphasis on earthing in health and wellness.

In Africa, the spiritual practice of earthing continues to thrive, reminding us of the deep-rooted connection between the Earth and the human spirit. As we look to the future, we can expect to see a greater integration of these spiritual practices into the global conversation on earthing, enriching our understanding and deepening our connection to the Earth.

Across the globe, the practice of earthing is being revived, reimagined, and reintegrated into our daily lives. From the forests of North America to the deserts of Africa, from the mountains of Asia to the plains of Australia, people are rediscovering the power of earthing and, in doing so, are rediscovering a part of themselves.

The future of earthing is a shared ground, a common soil that unites us in our diversity and reminds us of our shared humanity. As we move forward, let us do so with our feet firmly planted on the Earth, our hearts open to the wisdom of the ancients, and our minds attuned to the discoveries of the present. In this balance, this harmonious dance of energy and connection, we will find our true grounding.

## Chapter Summary

- Earthing, or grounding, is a universal practice that involves direct contact with the Earth's natural energy. It transcends geographical boundaries and cultural differences, uniting us all in a shared experience of the Earth's grounding energy.
- Indigenous cultures, such as the Aboriginal tribes of Australia and the Native Americans, have a deep-rooted connection with the Earth. They view the Earth as a living entity, a source of life, healing, and spiritual connection.
- Eastern philosophies, particularly those of China, India, and Japan, view the Earth as a source of life-giving energy. Practices like Tai Chi, Yoga, and Shinrin-yoku are seen as ways to connect with the Earth's energy and balance one's life force.
- In the West, the concept of earthing has been approached scientifically. Research has shown that regular grounding can reduce inflammation, improve sleep, increase energy, lower stress, and enhance the body's healing processes.

- African traditions view earthing as a spiritual practice. The Earth is seen as a spiritual entity, a source of life and wisdom, and earthing is often incorporated into spiritual rituals and ceremonies.
- The modern revival of earthing is a global trend driven by a growing body of scientific research and personal experiences of transformation and healing. People are rediscovering the grounding effects of direct contact with the Earth, seeking mental and emotional balance and physical benefits.
- The future of earthing lies in a shared understanding and unity. The wisdom of the ancients meets the discoveries of modern science, and the spiritual meets the physical in a harmonious dance of energy and connection.
- The resurgence of earthing in contemporary society is a testament to our innate longing for connection with the natural world. As we move forward, this connection will guide us, grounding us in the wisdom of the Earth and the energy of life itself.

# 8

---

# EARTHING AND ENVIRONMENTAL
# HEALTH

As we delve deeper into earthing and grounding, it becomes evident that the simple act of connecting with the Earth's surface extends beyond personal health benefits and touches upon a broader, more profound aspect of our existence: ecological awareness. At its core, earthing is an invitation to rekindle our relationship with the natural world. This relationship for many has been disturbed by the walls of modern living and the screens of digital devices.

Ecological awareness is rooted in the understanding that we are not separate entities from our environment but interconnected parts of a vast ecosystem. When we walk barefoot on the grass, stand under a tree's stretching branches, and immerse our hands in the rich, damp soil, we engage in a silent dialogue with the Earth. This dialogue is a reminder of the delicate balance that sustains all life on Earth.

Through the practice of earthing, we become more attuned to the delicate rhythms of nature. We start to notice the subtle changes in the quality of the air, the moisture in the soil, and the vibrancy of the plants around us. We develop a greater appreciation for the natural world and a stronger yearning to protect it. After all, the well-being of our planet is inextricably linked to our own.

Earthing encourages us to consider the impact of our actions on the environment. As we become more aware of the connectivity we share with the Earth, we may also grow more conscious of the activities that our modern lifestyles entail.

This awareness can inspire us to make more environmentally conscious choices, such as reducing energy consumption, opting for cleaner energy sources, and minimizing our reliance on technology that contributes to electromagnetic pollution. It can also lead to advocacy for more sustainable practices and policies that protect the Earth's integrity.

In essence, earthing is not just a personal health practice but a pathway to environmental stewardship. We can also ground ourselves philosophically by grounding ourselves physically, developing a more profound respect for the natural world and a commitment to its preservation. This shift in perspective is vital as we face the escalating challenges of climate change, biodiversity loss, and environmental degradation.

In the next section, we will explore how grounding practices can be integrated into a lifestyle that favors ecological balance and sustainability. This integration is beneficial for individual health and the planet's health as we learn to live in greater synergy with the natural world.

## Earthing and Sustainable Living

As we delve deeper into the interconnected relationship between earthing and the environment, we realize that the practice of earthing is not just beneficial for our well-being but also the sustainability of our planet. At its core, sustainable living is about making choices that ensure the health and well-being of both the environment and ourselves. Earthing, or grounding, aligns seamlessly with this philosophy by fostering a deeper connection between ourselves and Earth's natural systems.

Sustainable living encourages us to reduce our carbon footprint, conserve resources, and live harmoniously with the natural world. Earthing contributes to this lifestyle by reinforcing the importance of preserving the natural environment that provides this healing energy. When we walk barefoot on the Earth, we are not just receiving energy but also stepping into a relationship with the land that sustains us. This act can heighten our awareness of the land's condition and the impact of our actions upon it.

The practice of earthing can inspire us to adopt eco-friendly habits. For example, spending time in nature may lead to a greater appreciation for its beauty and a stronger desire to protect it. This could result in choices such as using fewer chemicals on our lawns and gardens, which not only allows for better conductivity with the Earth but also reduces the amount of harmful substances that seep into the soil and waterways.

In addition, the materials used for earthing products, such as conductive mats and sheets, can be designed with sustainability in mind. Manufacturers who prioritize eco-friendly production processes and materials help to minimize the environmental impact of these products. By choosing products made with natural and sustainable materials, we can support the environment while reaping the health benefits of grounding.

The principles of earthing can be integrated into the design and construction of eco-friendly homes and communities. By incorporating conductive materials and grounding technologies, these living spaces can be designed to facilitate regular earthing experiences, promoting both environmental health and personal well-being. This approach to architecture and community planning enhances the connection to the Earth and supports the broader goals of sustainable development.

In the context of sustainable living, earthing serves as a reminder of the intricate interdependence between our health and the health of our planet. It encourages us to live with greater environmental consciousness, understanding that the Earth is not merely a backdrop for human activity but a living system that we are a part of and responsible for. As we continue to explore the role of earthing in permaculture in the following section, we will see how these concepts can be practically applied to create self-sustaining and regenerative agricultural practices that honor and harness the Earth's natural energies.

## The Role of Earthing in Permaculture

Earthing finds a harmonious partnership in the embrace of permaculture. Permaculture—a contraction of "permanent agriculture"—is a philosophy and approach to land management that adopts arrangements observed in flourishing natural ecosystems. It is a design system characterized by its alignment with the patterns and resilient features of natural ecosystems. Earthing is pivotal in the permaculture ethos, enriching the land and those who tend to it.

At the heart of permaculture lies the principle of caring for the Earth, an ethos that resonates deeply with the practice of earthing. By walking barefoot on the soil, engaging in hands-on gardening, or utilizing grounding technologies, we can experience a direct connection with the Earth. This connection is not merely symbolic; it is a physical bonding that allows for the transfer of electrons from the ground into the body, promoting a sense of well-being and fostering a deeper understanding of the interconnectedness of life.

The role of earthing in permaculture extends beyond the individual to the land itself. Soil health is paramount in permaculture, and grounding practices can influence soil vitality. The Earth's natural electrical charge can affect the microbial life within the soil, which in turn supports plant growth and the overall health of the garden ecosystem. By maintaining a living connection with the ground, permaculture practitioners help ensure that the soil remains vibrant and full of life, essential for sustainable food production and ecological balance.

Moreover, earthing principles can be integrated into permaculture design through the conscious arrangement of plants and structures to enhance the natural energy flow. For instance, the placement of certain conductive plants or the use of water features can create a landscape that supports the ecosystem's health and facilitates grounding for humans and animals alike. This design approach recognizes the Earth as a source of healing energy that can be harnessed to benefit all living beings.

In permaculture, every element is carefully considered for its function and relationship to the whole. Earthing is no exception. It is a practice for individual health and a tool for building resilient and dynamic ecosystems. The grounding of both people and plants can lead to more robust and productive gardens, which in turn contribute to the health of the larger environment.

The integration of earthing into permaculture practices also serves as a reminder of the importance of observing and mimicking natural processes. Just as the Earth maintains a balance through its cycles and systems, permaculture seeks to emulate this balance in its designs, creating sustainable and nurturing spaces. Earthing reinforces this connection, grounding us in the understanding that human and environmental health are inextricably linked.

As we transition to the next section, let us carry the understanding that earthing is not only a personal health practice but also a vital component of environmental stewardship. Grounding ourselves is a tangible way to acknowledge and enhance our relationship with the natural world. This relationship is central to the permaculture philosophy and essential for the health of our planet.

## Connecting with Nature for Planetary Health

In the grand tapestry of our planet's health, each thread is interwoven with delicate precision, creating a balance that sustains all life forms. As we delve deeper into the practice of earthing, it becomes increasingly apparent that our connection with the Earth is not merely a pathway to individual well-being but also a vital link to the health of our planet. The Earth's surface is teeming with natural energies that can lead to profound environmental healing when engaged with respect and understanding.

Our planet is a living, breathing entity, and just like any organism, it requires care and nurturing. With its rapid technological advancements and urban sprawl, our modern lifestyle has led to a disconnection from the natural world. This detachment not only affects our health but also contributes to the degradation of the environment. Pollution, deforestation, and the exploitation of natural resources have resulted in a planet in distress. However, by reconnecting with nature through earthing, we can begin to reverse some of these adverse effects.

When we walk barefoot on the Earth, we do more than absorb the beneficial electrons that reduce inflammation and promote health. We also engage in an act of reciprocity with the environment. This practice encourages a greater awareness of the land beneath our feet—the soil that supports plant life, the grasses that feed the insects, and the ecosystems that depend on a delicate balance to thrive. By grounding ourselves, we become more attuned to the natural cycles and the environment's needs, fostering a sense of stewardship for the Earth.

Earthing can inspire a shift in how we interact with our surroundings. It can lead to more sustainable choices, such as adopting organic farming practices that honor the Earth's natural rhythms rather than depleting its resources. It can influence the materials we use, the food we consume, and how we manage waste. Through a grounded connection with the Earth, we can develop a deeper understanding of the impact of our actions and the importance of living in harmony with nature.

The health of our planet is inextricably linked to our own. When we ground ourselves, we not only draw healing energy from the Earth but also contribute to its restoration. Each step taken on the soft soil, each moment spent in contemplation of the natural world, is an opportunity to participate in the healing of our environment. As we nurture our connection with the Earth, we contribute to a collective effort to preserve the planet for future generations.

In this way, earthing transcends the realm of personal health and becomes a catalyst for environmental transformation. It is a practice that reminds us of our inherent connection to all living things and our responsibility to protect the intricate web of life. By grounding ourselves, we can foster a deeper respect for the Earth, leading to actions that support planetary health and ensure the vitality of our shared home.

As we move forward, let us carry with us the understanding that our relationship with the Earth is not one of dominion but of partnership. Through earthing, we can rekindle our bond with nature and work towards a future where the planet's health is seen as a reflection of our own.

## Chapter Summary

- Earthing and grounding reconnects us with the Earth, promoting ecological awareness, and reminding us of our interconnectedness with the environment.
- The practice of earthing attunes us to nature's rhythms, fostering a greater appreciation for the natural world and a desire to protect it.
- Earthing encourages environmentally conscious choices and sustainable practices, reducing our ecological footprint and electromagnetic pollution.
- The practice of earthing aligns with the concept of sustainable living, inspiring eco-friendly habits and choices in materials and products.
- Earthing principles can be integrated into eco-friendly architecture and community planning, enhancing environmental health and personal well-being.
- In permaculture, earthing enriches the land and those who tend to it, supporting soil health and the design of resilient ecosystems.
- Earthing in permaculture emphasizes observing natural processes, creating sustainable spaces, and recognizing the link between human and environmental health.
- The practice of earthing is a catalyst for environmental transformation, fostering stewardship for the Earth and encouraging a better contribution to planetary health.

# 9

# THE FUTURE OF EARTHING: TRENDS AND PREDICTIONS

A s we stand on the precipice of a new era, we find ourselves drawn back to the Earth, to the grounding energy that pulses beneath our feet. The journey towards a grounded future is not a new path but rather a rediscovery of an ancient practice, a return to our roots. It is a journey that beckons us to shed the shackles of our modern, disconnected lives and embrace the Earth's healing power.

In recent years, we have seen a resurgence in the popularity of earthing. From the sandy beaches of Australia to the lush forests of Scandinavia, people are rediscovering the benefits of connecting with the Earth. They feel the Earth's calming, healing energy and seek to incorporate earthing into their daily lives.

But the journey towards a grounded future is not without its challenges. As we move forward, we must navigate the complexities of our modern world, from the rapid pace of technological innovation to the looming threat of climate change. We must find ways to ground ourselves in urban landscapes, to connect with the Earth even when concrete and steel stand in our way. We must explore the role of earthing in future health and wellness trends, understanding how this ancient practice can contribute to our holistic well-being in the 21st century.

As we embark on this journey, let us remember that the Earth is not just beneath us but within us. It is a part of us, a part of our very being. And as we move towards a grounded future, let us embrace the Earth's energy, our connection to the Earth, and our holistic, grounded selves.

## The Rising Popularity of Earthing: A Global Perspective

As the sun rises, painting the sky with hues of orange and pink, a new day begins. Across the globe, from the bustling streets of Tokyo to the serene landscapes of rural Ireland, a quiet revolution is taking place. People are stepping barefoot on the Earth, feeling the cool dew-kissed grass beneath their feet, and connecting with the planet profoundly and primally. This is earthing, a practice as old as humanity itself, yet experiencing a resurgence in popularity that is nothing short of remarkable.

As we grapple with the stress and disconnection of our fast-paced lives, more and more people are turning to earthing to reconnect with nature and restore balance to their bodies and minds.

Earthing is gaining traction around the world. In the United States, a country often seen as the epicenter of modern lifestyle diseases, earthing is being embraced by a diverse range of individuals. Celebrities, athletes, and everyday people are all discovering the benefits of this simple yet powerful practice.

In Europe, the trend is equally evident. From the United Kingdom to Germany, people are increasingly seeking out green spaces to practice earthing, whether it's in city parks, private gardens, or the vast expanses of the countryside. The practice has also found a place in the wellness tourism industry, with retreats and wellness resorts incorporating earthing into their offerings.

With its rich history of holistic healing practices, Asia has also welcomed the earthing movement. In Japan, a country known for its deep respect for nature, earthing is being integrated into traditional practices like forest bathing or shinrin-yoku. In India, the birthplace of yoga, earthing is combined with this ancient practice to create a holistic wellness experience.

The rising popularity of earthing is a testament to our collective desire to reconnect with the Earth and restore balance to our lives. It is a global movement, transcending borders and cultures, uniting us in our shared need for connection and healing. As we look to the future, it is clear that earthing will continue to play a vital role in our journey towards a more grounded, holistic existence.

**Technological Innovations in Earthing Practices**

As we delve deeper into the future of earthing, it is impossible to over-look the role of technology in shaping and enhancing our connection with the Earth. The marriage of technology and earthing may seem para-doxical since earthing is fundamentally about returning to nature and disconnecting from our increasingly digital world. However, when used thoughtfully and responsibly, technology can be a powerful tool to deepen our understanding of the Earth and its energy and make earthing practices more accessible and practical.

One of the most significant technological innovations in earthing practices is the development of earthing or grounding mats. These devices, which can be placed under your feet or body, are designed to mimic the effects of walking barefoot on the Earth, even when you are indoors. They are connected to the Earth via a wire and a grounded wall outlet, allowing you to tap into its energy from the comfort of your home or office.

Another innovation is the advent of earthing shoes. Unlike traditional footwear, which often insulates us from the Earth, earthing shoes are made with conductive materials that allow the Earth's electrons to flow into our bodies. This means you can stay grounded even when walking on concrete or other artificial surfaces.

The rise of wearable technology has opened up new possibilities for monitoring and enhancing our earthing practices. For instance, some companies are now developing wearable devices that can measure your level of grounding in real time, providing you with immediate feedback and helping you to optimize your earthing experience.

However, as we embrace these technological innovations, it is crucial to remember that they are not replacements for direct contact with the Earth. Instead, they are tools that complement and enrich our earthing practices, especially in urban environments where direct contact with the Earth is often challenging.

In the future, we can expect to see even more technological innovations in earthing practices, driven by ongoing research into the health benefits of earthing and the growing demand for holistic wellness solutions. As we journey towards a more grounded future, technology will undoubtedly play an essential role in helping us to reconnect with the Earth and harness its healing energy.

## The Impact of Climate Change on Earthing

As we delve deeper into the future of earthing, we cannot ignore the looming specter of climate change. This global phenomenon, characterized by rising temperatures, erratic weather patterns, and a general disruption of natural ecosystems, has far-reaching implications for our relationship with the Earth.

Climate change, in its essence, is a disruption of the Earth's natural rhythms. It is a dissonance in the symphony of nature, a discord that reverberates through every aspect of our lives. As practitioners and advocates of earthing, we must acknowledge and address this disruption.

Earthing, at its core, is about connection. It is about grounding ourselves in the Earth's natural energy, tapping into the planet's primal pulse. But what happens when that pulse is disrupted? What happens when the rhythms we rely on become erratic and unpredictable?

The impact of climate change on earthing is multidimensional. On a physical level, changes in weather patterns can make it more challenging to practice earthing. Increased temperatures can make the ground too hot for barefoot contact, while increased rainfall can make it too wet and muddy. Extreme weather events, such as hurricanes and heat waves, can also disrupt our ability to connect with the Earth.

On a deeper level, climate change can disrupt the very energy we seek to tap into. The Earth's energy reflects its health, balance, and harmony. As climate change disrupts this balance, it can also disrupt the Earth's energy. This can make it more challenging to achieve the grounding and healing effects of earthing.

However, the challenges posed by climate change also present opportunities. They force us to innovate, adapt, and find new ways of connecting with the Earth. They push us to broaden our understanding of earthing to explore new practices and techniques.

They serve to remind us of the importance of our mission. Earthing is not just about personal wellness; it's about planetary wellness. It's about fostering a deeper connection with the Earth, about nurturing and protecting our planet. As we face the challenges of climate change, we are reminded of our vital role in this mission.

In the face of climate change, earthing takes on a new urgency. It becomes not just a practice but a call to action—a call to reconnect with the Earth, restore its rhythms, and heal its wounds. As we look to the future, we must embrace this call. We must ground ourselves in the Earth, not just for our wellness, but for the wellness of our planet.

## Earthing in Urban Landscapes: Challenges and Solutions

In the heart of the city, where concrete and steel dominate the landscape, the concept of earthing may seem like a distant dream. With its relentless pace and artificial structures, the urban environment poses a significant challenge to earthing. Yet, it is precisely in these bustling metropolises where the grounding effects of earthing are most needed.

The primary challenge lies in the need for direct contact with the Earth. High-rise buildings, paved streets, and the scarcity of green spaces create a physical barrier between city dwellers and the Earth's natural energy. The constant exposure to electromagnetic fields from electronic devices and Wi-Fi networks further disrupts our body's natural rhythms, increasing the need for grounding.

However, these challenges are not insurmountable. Innovative solutions are emerging to integrate earthing into urban lifestyles. One such solution is the development of earthing mats and sheets, which mimic the Earth's natural electrical charge and provide a means of grounding even in the city's heart.

Urban planning and architecture are also beginning to acknowledge the importance of earthing. Creating green spaces, rooftop gardens, and incorporating natural elements into building design are all steps towards a more grounded urban lifestyle. These initiatives provide city dwellers with a chance to connect with the Earth and contribute to the overall well-being of the urban environment.

Community initiatives, such as urban gardening and tree planting, also offer opportunities for earthing. These activities bring nature back into the city and foster a sense of community and connection, further enhancing the holistic benefits of earthing.

In the face of these challenges, the future of earthing in urban landscapes looks promising. As awareness grows and solutions evolve, city dwellers will have increasing opportunities to embrace the grounding benefits of earthing. The journey towards a grounded future is not limited to those with access to sprawling landscapes but is a path that can be tread even in the city's heart.

## The Role of Earthing in Future Health and Wellness Trends

As we journey deeper into the 21st century, the role of earthing in health and wellness trends is becoming increasingly significant. The world is gradually awakening to the profound benefits of this ancient practice, and its potential to shape our future health landscape is immense.

In the future, we can expect to see earthing integrated into a broader range of health and wellness practices. Already, it is being incorporated into yoga and meditation routines, with practitioners reporting enhanced relaxation and mindfulness. As our understanding of the Earth's energy and its impact on our health continues to grow, we can anticipate a surge in earthing-based therapies and treatments.

Scientific research will likely continually shape the future of earthing in health and wellness trends. As more studies are conducted into the physiological effects of earthing, we can expect to see a greater emphasis on grounding in preventative and curative healthcare. This could range from the use of earthing mats in hospitals to reduce patient recovery times to the promotion of regular grounding exercises as a means of preventing chronic diseases.

In the realm of mental health, earthing holds immense promise. The calming, grounding effect of connecting with the Earth can be a powerful tool in managing stress, anxiety, and depression. As our society grapples with a mental health crisis, earthing could offer a natural, accessible, and cost-effective solution.

The role of earthing in future health and wellness trends is set to be transformative. As we continue to explore and understand the Earth's energy, we will likely see a shift towards more holistic, grounded approaches to health and well-being. By embracing the power of earthing, we can look forward to a future where health is not just about treating illness but about nurturing a deep, sustaining connection with the natural world.

## Embracing the Earth's Energy for a Holistic Future

As we draw this exploration of earthing to a close, we find ourselves standing on the precipice of an exciting and uncertain future. The path that lies ahead is not without its challenges but also ripe with potential. It is a future that calls us to embrace the Earth's energy more holistically and meaningfully.

In all its raw and untamed beauty, the Earth has been our constant companion throughout the ages. It has nurtured us, sustained us, and shaped us in ways that are profound and far-reaching. And yet, in our relentless pursuit of progress, we have often overlooked the simple wisdom that the Earth offers. Earthing, as we have come to understand it, is not just a practice or a trend. It is a way of life, a philosophy that invites us to reconnect with the Earth and draw upon its energy to heal, rejuvenate, and thrive.

As we look towards the future, it is clear that earthing will play a pivotal role in shaping our health and wellness trends. The rising popularity of earthing and the advent of technological innovations have opened up new avenues for exploration and growth. From urban landscapes to the farthest corners of the globe, people are beginning to recognize the value of grounding themselves to the Earth.

However, the future of earthing is not without its challenges. Climate change, urbanization, and other global issues pose significant threats to our ability to connect meaningfully with the Earth. However, these challenges also present opportunities for innovation and adaptation. They push us to think creatively and to find new ways of grounding ourselves amidst the chaos and complexity of modern life.

In the end, the future of earthing is in our hands. We must embrace the Earth's energy, integrate it into our daily lives, and pass on this wisdom to future generations. It is a journey that requires courage, commitment, and a deep respect for the Earth and all its wonders.

As we step into this future, remember that earthing is not just about physically grounding ourselves. It is about grounding ourselves emotionally, spiritually, and mentally. It is about finding balance in a world that is often out of balance. It is about embracing the Earth's energy for a holistic future that is not just sustainable but also vibrant, healthy, and deeply connected to the rhythms of the Earth.

## Chapter Summary

- The practice of earthing, or grounding, is experiencing a resurgence as people globally seek to reconnect with the Earth's natural energy for its healing and calming effects.
- Despite the challenges posed by modern urban living and the rapid pace of technological innovation, earthing is becoming increasingly popular, with people finding innovative ways to incorporate it into their daily lives.

- Technological advancements, such as grounding mats and earthing shoes, are aiding in making earthing practices more accessible and effective, especially in urban environments.
- Climate change poses a significant challenge to earthing practices, disrupting the Earth's natural rhythms and energy. However, this also presents opportunities for innovation and adaptation in earthing practices.
- Urban landscapes present unique challenges to earthing due to the lack of direct contact with the Earth. However, solutions such as earthing mats, urban planning incorporating green spaces, and community initiatives make earthing possible in cities.
- Earthing is set to play a significant role in future health and wellness trends, integrating it into yoga, meditation, and potential use in healthcare for preventative and curative purposes.
- The mental health benefits of earthing, including stress and anxiety management, could offer a natural, accessible, and cost-effective solution to the current mental health crisis.
- The future of earthing requires holistically embracing the Earth's energy, integrating it into daily life, and passing on this wisdom to future generations. Despite challenges, earthing presents a path toward a future that is sustainable, vibrant, healthy, and deeply connected to the Earth's rhythms.

# 10

EARTHING'S CHALLENGES AND
CONTROVERSIES

I
n alternative health practices, earthing and grounding have sparked much debate. As we delve deeper into the scrutiny and skepticism around earthing, it becomes clear that we must approach the practice with a critical eye.

Some researchers and scientists have argued that much evidence supporting earthing is anecdotal or comes from studies with small sample sizes and methodological limitations. For example, while earlier chapters recounted numerous personal stories of transformation, these compelling narratives carry a different weight than controlled, peer-reviewed research. Concrete evidence must be presented before endorsing any health practice, and earthing is no exception.

Furthermore, the research that exists around earthing is often met with criticism regarding its experimental design. Issues such as lack of proper blinding, inadequate control groups, and potential conflicts of interest are highlighted, particularly when studies are funded by entities with a vested interest in earthing products. These factors can introduce bias and raise concerns about the validity of the findings.

Skeptics point out that the placebo effect could account for many of the positive outcomes reported by individuals while practicing earthing.

The placebo effect occurs when a person believes they are receiving a treatment and their symptoms improve despite the treatment having no therapeutic value. This psychological phenomenon is powerful and well-documented, and it can complicate the interpretation of subjective improvements in health.

Another point of contention is the biological plausibility of earthing's purported mechanisms. While it's true that the human body conducts electricity and that the Earth has a mild negative charge due to charged particles from the atmosphere, the leap to specific health benefits is not straightforward. Critics search for a clearer understanding of how this electrical interaction with the body's surface could influence complex physiological processes within the body.

Additionally, the scientific community often calls for a mechanistic explanation consistent with established principles of biology and physics. The body's electrical systems, such as the nervous system and the heart, operate on principles that are well understood, and any claims about earthing must be reconciled with these principles to gain broader acceptance.

Despite these challenges, research on earthing continues, with some studies suggesting potential benefits. However, the scientific community remains cautious until these findings are replicated in larger, more rigorous studies. The skepticism surrounding earthing is a reminder of the importance of maintaining scientific integrity and the need for continued investigation.

As we move forward to the next section, we will explore how the commercialization of earthing products and services has further complicated the conversation, raising questions about the integrity of the practice and the motives of those promoting it. It's a world where discernment is critical, and the true essence of earthing must not be lost to the siren call of profit.

## Navigating Commercialization and Integrity

In the burgeoning field of earthing, as with any wellness trend that captures the public's imagination, a delicate balance exists between commercial interest and preserving integrity. The promise of reconnecting with the Earth's natural electrical charge has inspired a new movement and spawned a growing product and service industry. This commercialization, while beneficial in spreading awareness and making earthing more accessible, also raises concerns about the dilution of the practice's core principles and the potential for consumer exploitation.

The growth of earthing products such as mats, sheets, and footwear has indeed made it easier for individuals to incorporate grounding into their daily lives, especially for those living in urban environments far away from natural landscapes. Often touted as channels to the Earth's healing energies, these products have been met with enthusiasm and skepticism. While they are a practical solution to modern lifestyle constraints, they are sometimes marketed with claims that stretch beyond the current scientific understanding, raising questions about their true efficacy and value.

As the earthing movement grows, consumers need to navigate this commercial landscape with a critical eye. It's wise to tread carefully and remember that the simplest form of earthing is just a barefoot walk on the ground. The shiny promise of well-marketed earthing products should be weighed against the simplicity of the practice's origins—barefoot contact with the Earth. While some products may offer convenience, they are not always necessary for effective grounding.

The essence of earthing lies in its accessibility and simplicity, and the commercial sector must be careful not to eclipse these virtues with overpriced and overhyped merchandise. Stakeholders within the earthing community must maintain a commitment to transparency, ensuring that products are responsibly marketed and backed by credible research where available.

This is not to suggest that all commercial ventures in the earthing space are inherently misleading. Many businesses are founded by passionate advocates who seek to improve people's health and well-being. These enterprises can play a vital role in supporting scientific research, developing innovative products that genuinely enhance the earthing experience, and educating the public about the benefits of grounding.

However, as with any industry, some may prioritize profit over principle. It is the responsibility of the earthing community—practitioners, researchers, and ethical businesses alike—to uphold standards that ensure the practice remains true to its roots. This includes fostering a culture of integrity where products are sold with honesty about their capabilities and limitations and where the noise of commercial gain does not obscure the primary message.

In conclusion, as earthing continues to captivate hearts and minds around the globe, it is the responsibility of all stakeholders to navigate the waters of commercialization with care and integrity. By putting the well-being of consumers and the Earth first, the earthing movement can flourish in a way that is true to its roots and respectful of the planet it celebrates.

## Legal and Regulatory Considerations

As we delve deeper into the complexities surrounding the practice of earthing, it becomes increasingly clear that the path to widespread acceptance is rife with scientific skepticism and legal and regulatory hurdles. These challenges are pivotal in understanding the journey of earthing from a fringe wellness practice to a potentially mainstream health recommendation.

The legal landscape for earthing is as varied as the terrain upon which one might walk barefoot. In the United States, the Food and Drug Administration (FDA) does not currently recognize earthing or grounding as a medical treatment at the time of writing, which means that products related to earthing cannot legally claim to diagnose, treat, cure, or prevent any disease without FDA approval. This presents a significant barrier for those wishing to market earthing products with health claims, as obtaining FDA approval is costly and time-consuming.

The regulatory environment is further complicated because earthing straddles the line between a lifestyle choice and a therapeutic intervention. If earthing products are categorized as medical devices, they would be subject to rigorous scrutiny and must meet specific safety and efficacy standards. However, suppose they are considered wellness or lifestyle products. In that case, they fall into a less stringent regulatory category, which, while easier to navigate, also limits the claims that can be made about their benefits.

The regulatory framework in the European Union (EU) is similarly complex. The EU's Medical Device Regulation (MDR) imposes strict rules on products claiming health benefits. To be legally sold within the EU, earthing products must comply with these regulations, including clinical evaluations and risk assessments. This presents a significant hurdle for earthing proponents seeking to expand their market reach.

Another legal consideration is the patent landscape. As earthing gains popularity, the potential for patent disputes increases. Inventors of earthing-related products may seek patents to protect their innovations, which could lead to legal battles over intellectual property rights. Such disputes can stifle innovation and make it more difficult for new earthing products to enter the market.

Additionally, there is the issue of liability. If an individual were to experience a negative outcome that they attribute to earthing practices or products, the legal considerations could be significant. Manufacturers and advocates should be cautious in how they promote earthing to mitigate the risk of lawsuits stemming from alleged injuries or health issues.

The legal and regulatory hurdles facing earthing are not insurmountable but require careful navigation. Earthing proponents must work within the existing legal framework to responsibly promote their practices and products. This includes conducting the appropriate scientific research to substantiate health claims and ensuring that marketing materials comply with the relevant advertising laws and regulations.

As we transition to the next section, which discusses the integration of earthing into medical practice, it's essential to consider how these legal and regulatory challenges influence the medical community's acceptance and implementation of earthing therapies. The journey of earthing from the ground beneath our feet to the halls of medical institutions is complex, and understanding the legalities involved is a crucial step in that journey.

## Earthing and Medical Practice

The concept of earthing has woven its way into the fabric of alternative medicine, allowing individuals to reconnect with the Earth's natural electric charge. Advocates suggest that such a connection can neutralize free radicals, reduce inflammation, and improve overall well-being. However, the integration of earthing into medical practice has been met with interest and skepticism, leading to a complex interplay between anecdotal success stories and the demand for rigorous scientific validation.

On one hand, some healthcare practitioners have embraced earthing as a complementary therapy. These practitioners often draw on the growing body of anecdotal evidence and preliminary scientific studies that suggest a range of health benefits. They argue that earthing offers a non-invasive, natural, and accessible means to potentially enhance patient care. For instance, some nurses have incorporated earthing techniques into patient recovery protocols, reporting improved sleep quality and reduced pain. Similarly, some physicians have recommended earthing mats or pads to patients suffering from chronic inflammatory conditions, noting positive changes in their patients' symptoms.

Despite these encouraging stories, the broader medical community remains cautious. The primary concern is the lack of large-scale, peer-reviewed studies that provide concrete evidence of earthing's efficacy. The medical field, grounded in evidence-based practice, requires rigorous research to substantiate therapeutic claims. Without this, earthing struggles to gain widespread acceptance and remains an outsider to conventional medical treatments.

Critics also point out that the physiological mechanisms proposed by earthing advocates need further investigation. The idea that grounding can influence the body's electrical state and thereby reduce inflammation is intriguing, but the mechanism and extent of these effects still need to be fully understood. This knowledge gap creates a barrier to integrating earthing into standard medical practice, where mechanisms of action are typically well-defined for accepted treatments.

Moreover, there is concern among the medical community about the potential for earthing to be seen as a panacea. There is a risk that individuals may prioritize grounding over established medical treatments, especially in the case of severe health conditions. This concern is compounded by marketing earthing products, which sometimes include bold claims unsupported by substantial scientific evidence.

The individualized nature of health and wellness further complicates the debate over earthing in medical practice. Health is a personal journey; what helps one person might not help another. This variability and the placebo effect make it hard to identify the actual benefits of earthing.

In conclusion, while earthing has found a place within certain corners of healthcare, it remains a subject of debate and scrutiny. The potential for earthing to contribute to patient care is an exciting prospect. Still, more research is necessary to understand its role fully and to establish guidelines for its use in medical practice. With a more robust scientific backing, earthing could one day find its place in healthcare.

**Future Earthing Research and Evidence**

As we venture into the realm of future research and evidence, it is crucial to acknowledge that the field of earthing and grounding is still in its infancy. Despite the growing body of anecdotal evidence and preliminary studies suggesting many health benefits, earthing remains a contentious topic within the scientific community. The skepticism largely stems from the need for more rigorous, well-designed research studies that can provide concrete evidence to support the claims made by earthing proponents.

The future of earthing research lies at a critical crossroads. To move beyond the challenges and controversies, researchers must embark on a path that adheres to the gold standards of scientific inquiry. This could involve conducting randomized controlled trials with larger sample sizes to test the effects of earthing on various health outcomes.

One of the critical areas for future exploration is the impact of earthing on inflammation. Inflammation is a common thread linking many chronic diseases, and earthing's potential anti-inflammatory effects are a central pillar of its proposed health benefits. Researchers must seek to quantify these effects and understand the pathways through which grounding may influence the body's inflammatory response. They need to measure, understand, and see it in action across different groups of people to make progress truly.

Another avenue for research is the exploration of earthing's effects on sleep and circadian rhythms. Sleep disorders and disturbances are rampant in modern society, and preliminary evidence suggests that grounding may improve sleep quality and normalize circadian rhythms.

The cardiovascular system is another area ripe for investigation. Early studies have indicated that earthing may influence blood flow, blood pressure, and heart rate variability. To build on these findings, researchers could conduct long-term studies to assess whether regular earthing practices can contribute to cardiovascular health and potentially reduce the risk of heart disease.

The psychological effects of earthing are an intriguing subject for future research. While personal stories have highlighted improvements in stress levels, mood, and overall well-being, empirical evidence is needed to substantiate these claims. Standardized assessments could paint a clearer picture of the psychological benefits of grounding and its impact on parameters such as stress, anxiety, and depression.

In addition to these specific health outcomes, future research could also address the practical aspects of earthing. How often should we earth, and for how long? Are all these products necessary, or can we get by with just the ground beneath our feet?

It is also essential for future studies to consider the potential placebo effect, which could contribute to the perceived benefits of earthing. By incorporating sham grounding as a control condition, researchers can better determine the actual effects of earthing.

Finally, as we look to the future, research in earthing must be conducted with transparency and a commitment to open science. By sharing data and methodologies, researchers can facilitate better studies and contribute to a more robust and credible evidence base. Only through collaboration and transparency can we overcome the challenges and controversies surrounding earthing and pave the way for a clearer understanding of its place in health and wellness.

**Chapter Summary**

- Earthing's empirical support is often anecdotal or from small, methodologically flawed studies, lacking the weight of controlled, peer-reviewed research.
- Positive outcomes from earthing could also be attributed to the placebo effect, where belief in treatment leads to perceived health improvements without therapeutic action.
- Existing earthing studies face criticism for issues like lack of blinding, inadequate control groups, and potential conflicts of interest, especially when earthing product entities fund such studies.
- Critics seek a clearer explanation of how earthing's electrical interactions with the body's surface could affect complex internal physiological processes.
- Claims about earthing must align with established biological and physical principles, particularly regarding the body's electrical systems.
- Despite making earthing more accessible, the commercialization of earthing products raises concerns about the dilution of earthing's core principles and potential consumer exploitation.

- Earthing faces challenges with FDA recognition and EU regulations, affecting how products can be marketed and the claims they can make.
- While some healthcare practitioners use earthing as a complementary therapy, the broader medical community requires more substantial evidence for widespread acceptance.
- Future research could focus on rigorous, well-designed studies exploring earthing's effects on inflammation, sleep, circadian rhythms, cardiovascular health, and psychological well-being while accounting for the placebo effect.

# EMBRACING THE EARTH'S EMBRACE

As we draw the curtain on this exploration of earthing, it is fitting to revisit our journey together. We embarked on this path with a simple premise: that the Earth beneath our feet, often taken for granted, holds a profound potential for healing and connection. We sought to understand the concept of earthing, delve into its roots, explore its branches, and see how it intertwines with our lives and well-being.

Our journey began with the basic understanding of earthing as a practice of grounding oneself to the Earth, of making direct contact with its surface. We explored the science behind this practice, the flow of electrons from the Earth into our bodies, and the potential benefits this exchange could bring. We delved into the history of our relationship with the Earth, tracing back to our ancestors who lived in harmony with nature, their feet firmly planted on the ground.

We then ventured into the heart of earthing, exploring how it can be integrated into our daily lives and the experiences of those who have embraced this practice. We heard stories of healing, transformation, and a renewed sense of connection to the Earth and oneself. We saw how earthing could serve as a bridge, linking the physical and the spiritual, the individual and the collective, the human and the Earth.

Throughout this journey, we have also grappled with the challenges and critiques of earthing. We have acknowledged the limitations of our current understanding, the gaps in our knowledge, and the need for further research. We have wrestled with the practicalities of earthing in our modern, urbanized world and the potential barriers to its widespread adoption.

As we stand at the end of this journey, we are not the same as when we began. We have unearthed a deeper understanding of earthing, its potential, and its challenges. We have seen the Earth not just as a passive surface beneath our feet but as an active participant in our lives, a source of healing and connection. We have felt the Earth's embrace, and in doing so, we have come to see ourselves and our place in the world in a new light.

In the following sections, we will delve deeper into our journey's major themes and findings, the implications and significance of earthing, and the limitations and critiques we have encountered. We will conclude with some final thoughts and recommendations as we look to the future of our relationship with the Earth.

## Unearthing the Core Insights

In this section, we delve into the heartwood of our exploration, unearthing the core insights that have emerged from our journey into the realm of earthing. These themes and findings, like the roots of a mighty oak, reach deep into the soil of our understanding, anchoring our knowledge and nourishing our perspective.

### Interconnectedness

The first central theme surfacing is the profound interconnectedness of all life. Earthing is not an isolated practice but a manifestation of the intricate web of relationships that bind us to the Earth and each other.

When we ground ourselves, we connect with the Earth's surface and the myriad forms of life that share our planetary home. This realization brings a sense of humility, a recognition of our place within the grand tapestry of existence.

## Transformative Power of Earthing

The second theme is the transformative power of earthing. Throughout our exploration, we have seen how this simple act can profoundly change physical health, emotional well-being, and spiritual awareness. From reducing inflammation and improving sleep to fostering a sense of calm and enhancing our connection with the natural world, the benefits of earthing are as diverse as they are significant.

## Accessibility

The third theme is the accessibility of earthing. Unlike many wellness practices, earthing does not require expensive equipment or specialized knowledge. It is a practice available to all, regardless of age, fitness level, or socioeconomic status. This democratization of wellness is a powerful reminder that the most effective healing practices are often the simplest and most natural.

## Resilience

Finally, we have discovered the theme of resilience. Earthing, we have found, is not just about grounding in the present moment but also about cultivating the strength and flexibility to weather life's storms. By connecting with the Earth, we tap into a source of stability and vitality that can sustain us through times of stress and change.

∼

These themes, while distinct, are deeply interwoven. They tell a story of connection, transformation, accessibility, and resilience—a story that is not just about earthing but about our relationship with the Earth and with ourselves. As we move forward, let us keep these insights close to our hearts, allowing them to guide us on our continued journey into the embrace of the Earth.

## Implications and Significance: The Ripple Effect of Grounding

As we delve into the third section of our concluding chapter, we find ourselves standing at the edge of a vast, interconnected web of implications and significance. This is where we begin to truly comprehend the ripple effect of grounding, the profound impact that earthing has on our lives and the world around us.

The act of grounding and physically connecting ourselves to the Earth is not merely a solitary act of self-care. It is a gesture of unity, a silent acknowledgment of our shared existence with the natural world. Each time we ground ourselves, we send out ripples of energy, vibrations that echo through the fabric of our lives and those around us.

The implications of grounding are manifold. On a personal level, grounding has been shown to promote physical and emotional well-being. It helps to reduce stress, improve sleep, and enhance overall vitality. It is a simple, accessible practice that can be incorporated into our daily routines, a gentle reminder of our inherent connection to the Earth.

On a broader scale, grounding fosters a sense of environmental stewardship. It reminds us of our responsibility to care for the Earth, to protect and preserve the natural world for future generations. It encourages us to live in harmony with nature and respect our ecosystem's delicate balance.

The significance of grounding extends even further, reaching into spirituality and philosophy. Grounding is a tangible expression of our interconnectedness, a physical manifestation of the spiritual concept that we are all one. It challenges us to reconsider our place in the universe and to question the artificial boundaries that separate us from the natural world.

However, grounding has its critiques and limitations, which we have explored. Despite these challenges, the practice of grounding holds immense potential. It offers a path towards greater health, harmony, and understanding, a way to nurture our bond with the Earth.

As we move forward, let us consider these implications and significance. Let us remember the ripple effect of grounding, the profound impact our actions can have on ourselves, our communities, and our world. Let us embrace the Earth's embrace, grounding ourselves in the knowledge that we are all part of the same beautiful, intricate web of life.

## Limitations and Critiques: The Unpaved Path of Earthing

As we tread further into the heart of this chapter, it is essential to acknowledge that the path of earthing, like any other, has its rough patches. The unpaved earthing path is strewn with limitations and critiques that we must address with an open mind and a willing spirit.

The first limitation we encountered was the need for more extensive scientific research on earthing. While preliminary studies have shown promising results, the field is still in its infancy. The effects of grounding on human health still need to be fully understood, and the mechanisms through which these effects occur remain primarily speculative. This lack of empirical evidence can make it challenging to convince skeptics of the benefits of earthing, and it also leaves room for misinterpretation and misinformation.

Another critique often leveled at earthing is its perceived impracticality. In our modern, urbanized world, many live in high-rise buildings and work in office environments where direct contact with the Earth is not always feasible. Critics argue that earthing is a luxury only those with access to natural environments can afford. However, this critique overlooks the various simple grounding techniques and tools used indoors, such as grounding mats and sheets.

The unpaved path of earthing also faces the challenge of commercialization. As earthing gains popularity, there is a risk that profit-driven motives could dilute its essence. The market is already flooded with many grounding products, some of which make exaggerated claims without substantial evidence. This commercialization can lead to skepticism and cynicism, potentially overshadowing the genuine benefits of earthing.

Lastly, there is a critique that earthing oversimplifies the complex nature of human health. Critics argue that grounding may contribute to well-being but is not a panacea for all health issues. It is crucial to remember that earthing is a complementary practice, not a substitute for professional medical advice and treatment.

Despite these limitations and critiques, the earthing path holds immense potential. It invites us to reconnect with our natural environment, listen to the subtle rhythms of the Earth, and rediscover nature's healing power. As we navigate this path, let us do so with humility, curiosity, and a deep respect for the Earth's wisdom.

## Nurturing the Bond with Earth

On this journey, we have delved into the heart of the Earth, felt its pulse beneath our bare feet, and discovered the profound impact it can have on our physical and emotional well-being.

In nurturing our bond with the Earth, we are not merely engaging in a passive act of connection. Instead, we actively participate in a symbiotic relationship, a dance of energy exchange as old as life. The Earth gives us life and sustains us, and in return, we must care for it, respect it, and honor its rhythms.

The practice of earthing is not a panacea for all ailments nor a substitute for medical treatment. However, it is a powerful tool in our wellness toolkit, a natural remedy that can complement and enhance our overall health and well-being. It is a gentle reminder of our inherent connection to the natural world, a connection that is often overlooked in our fast-paced, technology-driven lives.

As we move forward, I hope you continue exploring and deepening your relationship with the Earth. Make it a daily practice to walk barefoot on the grass, feel the Earth beneath your feet, and listen to its whispers in the rustling leaves and the murmuring streams. Allow yourself to be grounded, held, and nurtured by the Earth's embrace.

Remember, earthing is not a destination but a journey. It is a path of discovery, self-awareness, healing, and growth. It is a path that leads us back to our roots, true nature, and essence of who we are.

In conclusion, I invite you to embrace the Earth's embrace. Feel its energy, vitality, and life force flowing through you. To recognize and honor the sacred bond that exists between you and the Earth. To nurture this bond, cherish it, and let it guide you toward health, happiness, and holistic well-being.

May the Earth's embrace be your grounding force, healing balm, and constant companion on this beautiful journey we call life.

# ABOUT THE AUTHOR

Naomi Rohan is a devoted author and expert in natural wellness. With a deep-rooted passion for holistic health, she has dedicated her life to exploring and sharing the healing power of nature. Her books, which delve into topics such as forest bathing and earthing, have become essential reading for those seeking to reconnect with the natural world for their well-being.

Naomi's journey began with a degree in the field of natural sciences, which laid the foundation for her understanding of the intricate relationship between humans and nature. She further honed her knowledge through extensive travels, immersing herself in diverse cultures and their unique healing practices.

Naomi's work is characterized by her vivid, expressive writing style and ability to translate complex concepts into accessible, practical advice. She has a unique knack for guiding her readers on a journey of self-discovery and healing, helping them to find balance and harmony in their lives.

When she's not writing, Naomi can be found wandering in the woods, barefoot on the beach, or tending to her herb garden. She continues to be a student of nature, constantly learning, evolving, and sharing her wisdom with the world.

**FREE EBOOK BY NAOMI ROHAN: Nurtured by Nature**

Scan the QR code below to download your free copy of Nurtured by Nature:

Or visit:
https://teilingenpress.wixsite.com/home/naomi-rohan

www.ingramcontent.com/pod-product-compliance
Lightning Source LLC
Chambersburg PA
CBHW070124030426
42335CB00016B/2259